Stephan's Daughter

The Story of Rosa Siglaug Benediktson

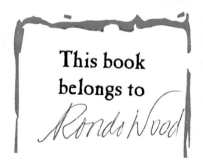

This book
belongs to

Rondo Wood

Joanne White

Published by:

Benson Ranch Inc.
251018 Tower Ridge Estates
Calgary, Alberta T2Z 2X8

This project was funded in part by the Alberta Historical Resources Foundation .

National Library of Canada Cataloguing in Publication Data

White, Joanne E., 1964-
Stephan's daughter : the story of Rosa Siglaug Benediktson
Joanne White.

Includes bibliographical references.
ISBN 0-9733657-0-6

1. Benediktson, Rosa Siglaug, 1900-1995.
2. Stephan G. Stephansson (Stephan Gu‾mundsson Stephansson), 1853-1927--Family.
3. Pioneers--Alberta--Biography.
4. Icelandic Canadians--Alberta--Biography.
I. Title.
FC3700.I3W44 2003   971.23'02'092   C2003-911173-3

Format and Layout by Joanne White in Macromedia® Freehand®10.
Cover Design by Joanne White.

Printed in Canada by Friesens Corporation

Table of Contents

Acknowledgments

I would like to thank the Benediktson and Stephansson families for introducing me to Rosa's story and for their generous and kind support throughout the process of writing this book. Rosa's son, Stephan Benediktson, got the whole project started by transcribing his mother's speeches and reminiscences. He and his sister, Iris Bourne, provided me with Rosa's papers and allowed me to delve into their many memories of their mother's life. Linda Benediktson, Marie Chaumont, and Edwin Stephenson also provided assistance in recounting many detail's of Rosa's story. *and Bill Bourne*

For her willingness to answer my numerous questions, I would like to thank Jane Ross, whose book *Stephan G. Stephansson: the Poet of the Rocky Mountains* was an invaluable resource. Thanks also go to Viðar Hreinsson, for taking the time to review the text and for assisting me with the Icelandic bibliographic references. In addition, I would like to thank Gary Duguay for helping me to find resources relating to the restoration of the Stephansson House Historic Site, and Michael Dawe for his reference assistance at the Red Deer and District Archives.

I gratefully acknowledge the many hours of copy-editing by Robert Wuetherick and Lorie White. I thank Erla Anderson for providing the translation of the many Icelandic letters that were among Rosa's papers. Thanks also to Bernice Anderson of the Stephan G. Stephansson Icelandic Society for answering my questions about the Fjallkona, and to Sandy J. Murray, President of Vonin Icelandic Ladies Aid, for permission to use material from the Vonin minute books.

I would especially like to thank Benson Ranch Inc. and the Alberta Historical Resources Foundation for their generous financial support, without which, this book could not have been completed.

Photographic Acknowledgments

All uncredited photographs in this volume came from the Benediktson family. Additional photographs and documents were courtesy of the Provincial Archives of Alberta, the Provincial Museum of Alberta Folk Life Collection, and the Old's College Alumni Association.

Foreword

More than twenty years ago after several years of documentation and restoration, Alberta Culture, Historic Sites Service, opened the farmstead of the Icelandic poet, Stephan G. Stephansson, to the public. It was a day of great celebration for the Icelandic community both here "in the west" and "at home" in Iceland. An important speaker that day was Rosa Benediktson. Rosa had long had a keen sense of her father's importance to Icelanders and Canadians alike and, as the youngest and only surviving child of the poet, she undertook the responsibility of representing her father at various occasions. The opening ceremonies that fine day of August 7, 1982 must have given her a great sense of satisfaction knowing that a quest begun years before had finally come to fruition.

It was a quest that had begun as a desire to have her father's poems translated into English thereby making them more accessible to Canadians. Although she made some initial inquiries into the feasibility of gathering and soliciting translations, she and others quickly realized the mammoth task that lay before them. Without dedicated time and money to undertake such a project, a comprehensive volume of Stephansson's translated works would have to wait. There was also a more pressing matter. The home where Rosa had been born and lived in until her marriage in 1928 had fallen into dereliction after the death of her brother Jakob in 1959. A hole in the roof threatened the integrity of the structure and by the 1970s the house was in a critical state of disrepair. Galvanized by the creation of Historic Sites Service in 1973, Rosa and the Icelandic clubs in Edmonton, Calgary and Markervillle pressed the government of Alberta to recognize Stephansson by declaring the homestead a Provincial Historic Resource.

A gift of money from the Icelandic Farmers Union in 1975 for the restoration of the house resulted in the creation of the Stephan G. Stephansson Homestead Restoration Committee. There were six members on the Committee.

Al Arnason and Ninna Campbell represented the Edmonton club; Cliff Marteinson and Bjorgvin Sigurdson were from the Leif Eriksson Club of Calgary, and Joe Johansson and, of course, Rosa represented the Icelandic community of Markerville. The Committee lobbied tirelessly to convince the government to work quickly to save the old homestead, and in 1978, as a senior research historian on staff of Historic Sites Service, I began researching Stephansson, the Icelandic communities in the west and the Stephansson farmstead. Over the next several years I worked closely with the Committee. If I needed translations of Stephansson's letters, I looked to Ninna Campbell and Bjorgvin Sigurdson. If I needed to meet old-time residents of the Markervillle area I traveled with "Little Joe" Johansson. The most important person on the committee to me as historian, though, was Rosa Benediktson. It was she who had the first-hand, intimate knowledge of her father and her old home. Although nearly 80 years of age, Rosa had a sharp, clear mind and her detailed memories of her father and mother, life on their farm, the landscaping around the home and the interior furnishings were critical to the accurate restoration of the house. I met with Rosa many times, sometimes in committee, sometimes by herself. On trips to the homestead we walked around the site and poked through the rooms, Rosa telling the stories behind the hops that grew profusely over the verandah, the newspapers that papered the pantry or the placement of furniture in each of the rooms while I furiously took notes. Rosa had waited and worked for the restoration of her father's home for many years and, while always gracious, she nevertheless knew what she wanted. Even after the house was restored and opened to the public, Rosa continued for a number of years to be a valuable resource for the interpretative staff of Historic Sites Service.

The necessary emphasis on Stephansson has, nevertheless, left many gaps in the story. For example, we know relatively little about Helga Stephansson, Rosa's mother, or about Rosa's siblings. And, until now, we have known little about Rosa herself. Joanne White's organization of Rosa's papers and photographs has brought to light the life of a woman whose life spanned nearly a century. Born into a tight-knit Icelandic society, Rosa married within her community. That community, though, was in the throes of change. Better roads and communication broke down the isolation of the homesteads. More opportunities for higher education and jobs meant that many in the Markerville area left. Rosa's children married outside their ethnic boundaries.

None took over the family farm. Rosa herself eventually left the farm to work in Red Deer in a much larger, mainstream society. Resilient, she adapted, but she never forgot her roots, a heritage to which she was able to return late in life. This is her story, one which mirrors the changes that the Icelandic - and other ethnic communities - have had to face and accept while keeping the memory of their language and culture.

Jane Ross
Curator, Western Canadian History
Provincial Museum of Alberta

Pink paint on a small
bit of board resulted in
the house being painted
pink in approx 1980.

Introduction

In order to fully understand the story of Rosa Siglaug Benediktson (nee Stephansson) one must know something of her famous father, Icelandic-Canadian poet Stephan G. Stephansson. Stephansson was a prolific writer whose work in his native Icelandic is treasured in his homeland and among his fellow "Western Icelanders" in Canada and the United States. His hundreds of poems and letters have been published in many volumes in Icelandic and English, receiving praise for more than a century. In addition to his literary contribution, Stephansson was a true pioneer, homesteading in Wisconsin in 1873, North Dakota in 1880, and finally in central Alberta in 1889, where he contributed to the development of the Icelandic community in the Markerville area, southwest of Red Deer.

Although it may be tempting to delve into the poetry of Stephan G. Stephansson or to recount his many other achievements, the focus of this publication is the story of his youngest daughter, Rosa, and her own accomplishments. Throughout her life, Rosa wrote about her family and her experiences growing up in Alberta. In her later years she was often asked to speak about her heritage and she became an important representative of her community. It will largely be left up to Rosa to tell her own story through those narratives and addresses, however, there were times in her life that she did not write as much, for instance when she was away at college or busy raising children. Fortunately, she saved many photos, letters and other documents that help to illustrate those periods of her life.

Rosa's story begins long before she was born, with the emigration of her parents to the U.S. and then Canada. It describes her life as a child on a prairie farm and as one of the first young women to attend Alberta's new agricultural college at Olds. The story continues with her marriage to Sigurdur Benediktson, the birth of her four children, and the tragic early death of her husband. As international interest in her father's work increased, she began to take on the privilege and responsibility of preserving his legacy, both by assisting scholars with the publication of his poetry and letters, and later advising on the restoration of her family home, Stephansson House, now a Provincial Historic Site.

Much of the written Stephansson legacy is preserved in Icelandic, although Rosa's own work was primarily in English. The letters from family and friends that appear in the book have been translated into English, but the occasional word or phrase has been given a broader explanation where direct translation has been difficult. English spellings have been used in the text in most instances.

Some choices of spelling are more problematic than others. Even within the Stephansson family, different anglicized spellings occurred. The most common of these is the Icelandic "ð". The closest pronunciation for this in English is the "th" sound, as in "the", and it is often translated using "th". In Rosa's writings, she chose to spell it with the English "d", so for consistency that spelling will be used here. An example of this is the Icelandic spelling of "Guðmundur", Stephan's father's name. Although often spelled "Guthmundur", the most common family spelling is "Gudmundur". Similarly, her grandmother's name "Guðbjörg" is spelled as "Gudbjorg". Another example of alternate spelling occurs with Rosa's sister's name. Her English name was "Jennie"; one Icelandic spelling is "Jóny"; however, both she and her father spelled it "Jóna". In the text she is referred to as both "Jona" and "Jennie".

Stephan's own name underwent several changes in his lifetime. He was born "Stefán Guðmundsson". On his arrival in America, officials mistakenly gave him his father's surname, so he became "Stefán Guðmundsson Stefánsson".[1] He later anglicized it to "Stephan Gudmundson Stephansson". As a writer he became known simply as "Stephan G.", and that shorter form has been used throughout the publication.

The gradual shift from Icelandic to English spellings reflects the gradual acculturation of the Western Icelanders. Rosa's life spanned two very different cultures and, in a way, two very different times. Her early life as part of a rural farming community was far distant from her later life of world travel and public speaking. Rosa perhaps would be surprised to know that her writing and all of the letters and articles that she saved would one day provide an invaluable look into the history of one pioneering Alberta family and the Icelandic Canadian community that they helped to create.

The Journey

Rosa was extremely proud of her Icelandic roots and the pioneering accomplishments of her parents and grandparents. Many times throughout this volume she relates the story of her parents and the other Western Icelanders who carved homes out of the North American wilderness, not once but three times. Because her accounts are often brief, relating only certain aspects of the journey, an overview of the story may be useful to fill in some details.

Rosa's parents were first cousins who had known each other in Iceland when they were young. Stefan Gudmundsson was born in the Skagafjordur region of Northern Iceland, on October 3, 1853. His family rented a number of farms in the area until financial difficulties forced them to move again in 1870, this time to live and work with his father's half sister Sigurbjorg and her husband Jon Jonsson, the parents of his future bride, Helga.[1] By 1873, several years of poor weather and volcanic activity had made the economic situation increasingly intolerable for many Icelandic farmers, and finally both families made the difficult decision to leave Iceland and emigrate to Wisconsin.[2] The party included Stephan G.'s parents, Gudmundur Stefansson and Gudbjorg Hannesdottir, his sister Sigurlaug, his aunt Sigurbjorg Stefansdottir and her husband Jon Jonsson; fourteen-year-old Helga, and her younger brother Jon. One hundred and sixty-five passengers left Iceland for North America but only fifty Icelanders went as far as Wisconsin.[3] While in Wisconsin, Stephan G. and Helga were married near Green Bay on August 24, 1878. He was twenty-four and she was nineteen. Their first son, Baldur, was born in 1879, and the following year the families again decided to move on, this time to North Dakota.

The Dakota years were filled with both joy and tragedy. In 1881, Stephan G.'s father died, only one month before the birth of Gudmundur, named in honour of his grandfather. The couple's third son, Jon, was born in 1883, followed by Jakob in 1886. A year later however, tragedy struck again in the form of a diphtheria epidemic. All three children became ill, and three-year-old Jon died. Stephan G. poured out his grief in a series of poems written over the next several years.[4]

By 1889, the Stephanssons were ready to leave Dakota, but they were not the first Western Icelanders to make this decision. A year before, in the spring of 1888, a group voted to send Sigurdur Bjornson ahead to find land in Canada. Nine families and three single men made the trip north, stopping in Winnipeg to buy supplies. Winnipeg was home to many Icelandic settlers, and two more families and another young man, decided to join the group heading west. Continuing on to Alberta, they finally travelled north to the Red Deer River. After a failed attempt to ford the river using horses, the settlers built a flat ferry and successfully crossed.[5]

"The next day, the 28th of June [1888], the men started looking around. Everybody had had enough traveling and wanted to settle down. They scattered far and wide looking for suitable places to build. Some went farther than necessary, for they found it hard to work together when they were so far apart. Now after ten years it gives me the shivers to think back at the situation then. To be out there with women and children, altogether penniless in a wild country, 100 miles from civilization and the comforts of life. It was awful and for a long time many paid for the dream that brought them out here. But on the other hand, it was marvelous how everything went and how well all of the obstacles and hardships were conquered by those first pioneers." Jonas J. Hunford, 1909 [6]

The new community founded by these pioneers was called Tindastoll, near what became the town of Markerville, shown here ca. 1910

When the Stephansson party arrived, they too settled on the north side of the Red Deer River, just east of the Medicine River. Twin daughters Stephany (Fanny) and Jona (Jennie) were born at their new home in 1890 and a fifth son, Gestur, was born in 1893. The land that the Stephanssons occupied was not surveyed until 1896, and Stephan G. did not officially file for his land until 1898. His quarter was slough land, which was chosen for hay. It was located in the northeast corner of Section 22, Township 37, Range 2.[7] As a widow, Stephan G.'s mother, Gudbjorg, was entitled to land of her own, and in 1902 she received the patent for the southeast quarter of Section 10. Although Stephan G. had built a small home on his quarter to establish residency, it was Gudbjorg's land further south that became the family homestead.[8]

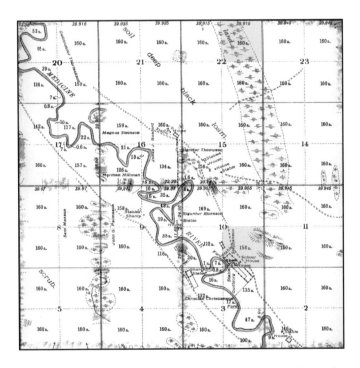

This 1887 map of a portion of Township 37, Range 2, shows the two quarter sections filed on by Stephan G. and his mother, Gudbjorg (shaded) Provincial Archives of Alberta, 83.421

Rosa, born in July of 1900, was told often of her family's journey by both her parents and grandmother, but she herself recounted only portions of the story. The first of Rosa's speeches printed in this volume was written for an anniversary of her grandmother, Gudbjorg, although the exact occasion is unknown. In the speech she briefly relates the early part of the journey and the final settlement of the family in Alberta. In her essay "From Wisconsin to North Dakota to Alberta" she fills in some details about their time in North Dakota. Throughout this volume, however, she returns to the story in several written accounts and public addresses.

Crossing the Medicine River, ca. 1909

Looking north from the family homestead

Speech for an Anniversary of Gudbjorg Hannesdottir
Rosa - no date

It gives me a great deal of pleasure to be here on this momentous occasion having had the good fortune to be born in our lovely Alberta and having resided here all my life.

All four of my grandparents came from the northern part of Iceland, each with two children, to the state of Wisconsin in the United States in 1873. I thought perhaps that since you might not be familiar with Iceland, it would perhaps be in order to tell you a bit about the country. Iceland is the second largest island in Europe, about 300 miles from east to west and about 190 miles from north to south. The island is located close to the Arctic Circle and has a frigid sounding name but the climate is much milder than you would expect. The warm Gulf Stream current flows around the south and west coasts. Unlike Canada, the rivers in the south do not freeze over. It is a very scenic country, mountainous with grass growing up the mountainsides, many hot springs and geysers and waterfalls in the coastal regions. The capital city of Reykjavik has a unique heating system; the city is heated with natural hot water brought in a distance of some ten miles. As a result there is no pollution. I am proud to say that an engineer from Winnipeg, a Western Icelander engineered the project.

My mother's parents had a good farm in northern Iceland and were relatively prosperous whereas my father's parents had not acquired very much. My maternal grandfather and my paternal grandmother were brother and sister. The decision to leave was made. The first leg of the journey from Iceland to Glasgow was on a boat carrying a cargo of horses and the accommodation left much to be desired. As a result most of the passengers became seasick. My father took it well and was able to assist the passengers. He had acquired some knowledge of English, which was a great asset.

They landed at Granton, Scotland and had to travel by rail to Glasgow where they boarded a second ship bound for the New World. The accommodations on the second ship were much better. When they sailed up the mighty St. Lawrence River they had to make a decision to go to Canada or the United States and they chose the latter and decided to go to Wisconsin. They travelled to Milwaukee, Wisconsin by train and enroute they were in a railway collision which resulted in some deaths but fortunately the Icelandic group escaped with minor injuries.

My parents and their families lived in Wisconsin with the Icelandic group for seven years. They were married and started their family there. They lived in a largely Norwegian settlement and learned to speak Norwegian. I remember my father saying how he enjoyed going to the garden to partake of a cool watermelon after a hot day's work in Wisconsin. The rich soil would grow almost anything from pumpkins to tobacco. The huge hardwood forests were hard to clear for cultivation however, so when they heard of the fertile plains of North Dakota the group of Icelanders decided to migrate there. The women and children and some men went by train while the balance went by horseback and on foot driving their livestock, a distance of almost 1000 miles.

After sixteen years in the United States, in 1889 my parents moved to Alberta, then called the Northwest Territories, with their three sons and my grandmother. The family stayed in Calgary which was then the end of the railroad, while father went to pick a homestead and build a house for his family. As my grandmother was widowed in North Dakota, she also had homestead rights so my father filed on two properties, the one where Stephansson House stands he filed on for my grandmother and some distance to the north east he filed on grassland for himself. We are today celebrating the anniversary of my paternal grandmother, Gudbjorg. She was born July 8, 1830 in northern Iceland and died on January 12, 1911, at the age of 81 years at her home here. She always made her home with my parents and her only daughter lived nearby, their entire lives. Grandmother was an honored member of the family and had two rooms to her disposal. As she became more frail she stayed in her room and my mother served her coffee and meals there. I remember my father summoning Dr. R. Parsons Sr. to examine her. He said, "Continue as you have been doing to care for her. She is worn out and I have no cure for that."

Rosa's paternal grandmother Gudbjorg Hannesdottir

There were no good building logs on the land my father selected so he had to go farther north and west for them and float them down the river. It took until August for father to make things ready and return to Calgary for his family. They travelled the 100 miles to the present home site, which became the family home from that time on. On October 6th of that year my parents were blessed with twin girls, one with black hair and brown eyes and one with fair hair and blue eyes. The house today is an historic site. It was added to and improved until 1905 to its present form.

My father had no formal education in English, except for a little instruction before he left Iceland. Nevertheless he was able to interpret for his countrymen on the journey to America. My father spent the first summer with a survey crew in the wilds of Alberta, in order to supplement the family income. I note from his letters that he was very taken with the land near Edmonton and thought of moving there, but nothing came of it. My father always had some extra work, besides farming. He was the census taker, the Commissioner of

Oaths and people often came to him to have him write important letters. His handwriting was so very legible, although he had no formal education. Father was Secretary-Treasurer of the first school in the district and of the Markerville Creamery which he helped establish. He always ably supported all projects that benefitted the community.

My father had a great poetic gift. After working on the farm all day, he would sit up at nights composing poetry. With the help of friends, his poems were published in six volumes, two volumes in 1909, two in 1910, one in 1923 and one posthumously. He called them "Wakeful Nights". He wrote all his poetry in the Icelandic language, although he was fluent in English. Some have been translated into English. My father was a great humanitarian and abhorred war and violence of any nature. My mother had old love poems, which he had composed to her before they were married, published 60 years later. They illustrate his deep emotions. Although the poetry was in a lighter vein, the poems illustrate another side of his nature. He wanted education for his children as testified by the fact that he was one of the principle instigators in the formation of a school for the community. To me, it is very gratifying to know how deeply he has touched the lives and brought comfort to so many through his poetry.

My father died on August 10th, 1927. My mother outlived him by 13 years. She was a great helpmate for him. A very fine wife and mother. She worked hard during the pioneering days and always had her family's interests at heart. They are both buried in our family cemetery, across the river from our old home. My father had a cenotaph erected to his memory there, by friends and family, another one in the park at Markerville and one in Iceland near his birthplace.

Thank you all.

From Wisconsin to
North Dakota to Alberta
Rosa - no date

In 1880, a party of Icelandic immigrants, who had been struggling for seven years to hew out an existence from the wooded areas of Shawano County, Wisconsin, decided to immigrate to North Dakota in the hope of finding a location more suitable for them. They had tired of the back breaking task of cutting down the huge hardwood forests to establish farms. Among them were a young couple, Stephan G. Stephansson and his young wife and their son. Helga Johnson and Stephan G. had been married at Green Bay, Wisconsin, on August 28, 1878.

As funds were low and they were unwilling to part with what little livestock they had it was decided that the women and children would go by train and the men would drive the cattle on foot, a distance of 800 some miles. It seemed a big task, but it was accomplished. The older men took it upon their shoulders to do that whilst the younger men, Stephan G. and his brother-in-law Jon Johnson and some others went earlier in the year to secure work. The women and children went by train and arrived at their destination, which was Crookston, North Dakota.

They were met by Stephan G. who had secured some work there. From there Stephan G., Helga and their son Baldur went to Pembina, where they stayed for a couple of days. From there they went to their location which was a few miles from the present hamlet of Gardar. There Helga, her young son and the grandmother got permission to stay in a small shack while Stephan G. was building on their own place. By fall a log house had been erected and meanwhile the older men had arrived with the livestock after two and one half months of travel. Preparations were made for winter.

Stephan G. purchased another quarter of land and built a good log house on it but later sold it and moved back to his first homestead where the family lived during their entire stay of nine years in Dakota.

Three sons were born to Helga and Stephan G. in Dakota; Gudmunder on the 9th of December, 1881 and Jon in 1883 and Jakob Kristinn on the 8th of June, 1886. Sorrow visited the pioneer home in the winter of [1887]. A sickness had been in the neighborhood and the three boys got it. Doctors and medical aid were hard to procure, but were sent for to no avail. Jon succumbed to the disease, which proved to be the dreaded disease diphtheria. Helga struggled on working hard to keep her family and home as best she could. The lot of these pioneer women was no easy task.

In 1889, Stephan G. decided to emigrate once more and so this time the destination was Alberta, Canada. The grandmother, Helga, Stephan G. and the three boys boarded the train, after having sold their land. With their few head of livestock and some equipment they arrived in Calgary in May, in a blinding snow storm. That was the end of the railroad then. The family stayed two months in Calgary while Stephan G. had gone on 100 miles north west of Calgary to locate a homestead. Then came the day when the family must adjourn out to the homestead. Helga with her three sons boarded the prairie schooner, a yoke of oxen being the power, and the long trek was begun. A person can well imagine what that trip would be like for a woman.

Baldur, Gudmundur, and Jakob, North Dakota, 1888
Provincial Museum of Alberta PH75.28.3

The earliest photo of the Stephansson Family Home, ca. 1900

Childhood

L to R: Gestur, Gudmundur, Jakob, Stephany, Baldur, and Jona, with Rosa in front, 1907

Being the youngest of a large family, Siglaug Rosa Stephansson grew up in a very busy household. Rosa was born at the home of her parents on July 24th, 1900, delivered by her Aunt, Sigurlaug Christinnson, who was a mid-wife. Tanta, as she was called, was Rosa's namesake, and the two always had a close relationship. According to Tanta, Rosa was a very small baby, weighing possibly only three and a half pounds. In spite of Rosa's small size, Helga took her new baby to her first Icelandic picnic, on August 2nd, 1900.[1]

The first few years of Rosa's life were spent with four brothers, Baldur, Gudmundur (Mundi), Jakob (Jake or Kobbi), Gestur, and twin sisters Stephany (Fanny) and Jona (Jennie). Her paternal grandmother, or "amma", Gudbjorg Hannesdottir, also lived with the family until her death in 1911. Gudbjorg was an important figure in the lives of the children, teaching them Icelandic and helping with the farm and household work as long as she was able. Although Rosa's oldest brothers, Baldur and Mundi, married when she was still very young, they remained nearby and visited often. The family also had close ties to Tanta (Sigurlaug) and the Christinnson cousins, who lived just across the Medicine River.

The community in which she lived was close-knit, with her father playing an important role in its development. He helped to establish the Tindastoll Post Office in 1892, and both the Tindastoll and Hola Schools a year later.[2] Stephan G. hosted many meetings at the family home, and visitors came to the house regularly, often having discussions in his study that lasted long into the evening. Travel was sometimes difficult, so it was not uncommon to have visitors stay the night, or in bad weather, for several days. A number of teachers lived in the house for weeks or months due to the location of Hola school on the Stephansson property. Rosa's diary, which covers the first three months of 1916, gives a glimpse into the comings and goings of the Stephansson household as she was growing up.

Her oldest brother, Baldur, was already twenty when she was born, and even her closest sibling, Gestur, was seven years older than Rosa. Her brother Jake, who was fourteen years her senior, had already taken over much of the running of the farm by the time she started school. Rosa was a bright girl who liked school. As a much younger child with somewhat less responsibility than her siblings, she was perhaps more able to devote time to studying and reading.

Education was of the utmost importance to the Western Icelanders, and Rosa's household was always supplied with books, either from school or from the library in Markerville, which was established in 1892 by the Lestrarfelagith Ithunn, or "Debating Society of Ithunn".[3] Stephan G. was actively involved in the creation of both the society and the library. He also had a small but precious collection of books in his own study.

Rosa always had the greatest respect for the written word. Early on, she began a lifelong habit of clipping stories, poems, and articles from magazines and newpapers. Many of the items that she pasted into an old school book were from the *Canadian Teacher* magazine, possibly supplied by her own school teacher.

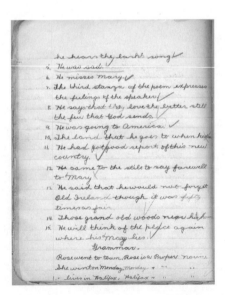

Rosa carefully pasted clippings from magazines into one of her old school books.

The greatest tragedy of Rosa's young life was the death of her brother Gestur. Only a couple of weeks before her ninth birthday, in July of 1909, he was killed when he touched a barbed-wire fence that had been electrified by a lightening strike. Much has been written about her father's grief, expressed in his poem "Gestur". Her parents had already lost their three-year-old son Jon to diphtheria while still in North Dakota. Gestur was only sixteen at the time of his death. It was a terrible blow to the family.

Rosa's accounts of her childhood provide only a small amount of insight into her own relationship with her father, however her great respect and affection for him are evident in all of her writing and speeches. He was already forty-six years old when she was born; by that time in his life he was spending more and more time with his writing and speaking engagements. In a filmed interview in 1978 she recalled some special moments with her father when she would slip into his study late at night while he was working. Little was said between them, but she was allowed to sit quietly and watch him work until she was ready to return to bed.[4] In the summer of 1926, one year before his death, Rosa accompanied her father on a trip to Wynyard (Saskatchewan) and North Dakota.

The Wynyard newspaper, *The Advance*, reported: "Stephan G. Stephansson of Markerville, Alta., with his daughter Rosa, last Saturday concluded a ten days visit to Wynyard, and the neighborhood. In May, this year, Mr. Stephansson went to Winnipeg for medical advice and treatment and while resident in the city he has made several trips to the Icelandic communities in North Dakota and Manitoba renewing aquaintance with a number of his admirers."[5]

Rosa at her Father's homestead in North Dakota, 1926

Rosa wrote fondly about her memories of growing up. Her article "My Parents", published as "Foreldrar Minir" in the Icelandic series *Vestur i frumbyli* [6], gives yet another account of her parents' arrival in Alberta. It also provides the small details that help to draw a real picture of the people she loved. It is one of the few places where the relationship between Stephan G. and Helga is revealed. Their years of struggle and loss and Helga's support of his work illustrate their strong bond and commitment to each other.

While her narrative "Our Horses" and her speech for the "Hola School 75th Anniversary Celebration" give some additional insight into her childhood, perhaps the most telling of her writings is her own diary. Written in the early part of 1916, when she was fifteen years of age, "My Diary" provides a wonderful account of her daily life. Her small tight script was carefully written in a pocket calendar. For the rest of her life she continued this practive of writing all of her speeches and notes in small booklets.

In transcribing the diary, every effort was made to leave her spelling and syntax as it was originally written. Her youthful style would be lost if corrections were made; however, there are a number of points that require clarification. Her spelling was inconsistent at times. Early in the diary, to-day and to-night were written with hyphens which later became a horizontal extension of the written "o", and then disappeared altogether. Even the spelling of names changed: Jennie was sometimes spelled Jenny, and Arni changed to Arney. She also used several abbreviations such as "M'ville" for Markerville and "T" for Teacher. On several occasions she refers to "La Grippe", a flu-like virus that was going around. At first, not understanding the French article and only hearing it spoken by others, she calls it "the La Grippe", and later, just "the Grippe".

Hola Bridge looking east toward Hola school and the Stephansson farm

Left: This photo was taken at Mundi's wedding to Regina Strong (seated), in January, 1905. Baldur (left) was the best man, and his future bride, Sigurlena Bardal, was bridesmaid.
Provincial Museum of Alberta, PH75.28.13

Below: Rosa's Public School Leaving Diploma, dated October 15, 1915

So many individuals are mentioned in the the diary text that it is impossible to identify them all. A few, however, should be mentioned. Sigurlena Bardal married Baldur in December of 1905. Fanny married Arni Bardal in 1917 and Jennie married Siggi Sigurdson in 1922 (see photo pg. 39). Frost was one of the Christinnson cousins who lived across the river. The Hunford's were an important Markerville family. Jonas J. Hunford was an early settler who wrote several accounts of the arrival of the Western Icelanders in the area. His son Jon or "John" also appears in the diary.

In 1915, a year before her diary was written, Rosa received her Public School Leaving Diploma. Although she had completed the mandatory eighth grade, Rosa chose to remain in school. She then went on to further education in 1919, when she left home for the first time to attend the Alberta School of Agriculture in Olds, studying Home Economics. Returning in 1921, Rosa again lived on the family farm until a year after her father's death in 1927, when she married another Western Icelander, Sigurdur Vilberg Benediktson.

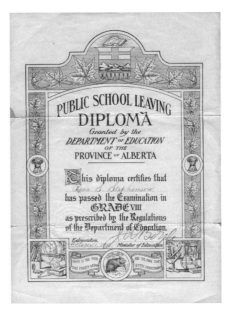

Rosa's article "My Parents" was first printed under the title "Foreldrar Minir" in Reykjavik in 1956. It was published by Finnbogi Gudmundsson, who held the first Icelandic Chair at the University of Manitoba, later returning to Reykjavik, where he became head of the National Library of Iceland.[7] This English version of "My Parents" was translated by Ninna Campbell from the Icelandic text, as published in *Vestur i frumbyli*, Reykjavik 1989.

Stephan G. in 1909
Provincial Museum of Alberta
PH75.28.15

Helga at Home

**Helga and Stephan G., after he
had suffered a stroke in 1926**

My Parents
Rosa - 1956

My father was Stephan Gudmundsson, son of Gudmundur Stefansson and his wife Gudbjorg Hannesdottir. My mother was Helga Jonsdottir, daughter of Jon Jonsson and his wife Sigurbjorg Gudmundsdottir. All these people moved to America together in the year 1873, from Bardardal in Sudur-Thingeyrarsysla, in the north of Iceland.

I think my first memory of my father was in connection with "Ash Day," and I was very young then. Having heard that people had to bear ashes on that day, I put some ashes in my father's shoes. I remember that he spoke seriously to me and expressed his disapproval, which still sticks in my memory.

The picture becomes clearer and I visualize a rather short and slender man, stooped at the shoulders and showing signs of having worked hard over the years. His face was rough-hewn and he had a high forehead. His hair was dark, with grey streaks. When he was 18 he had lost a lot of his hair. He had a reddish moustache but it was his eyes that were most memorable. They were blue, sharp and deep set, and when he grinned, they seemed to twinkle. He had a serious appearance, was never boisterous, but when spoken to he always responded in the same agreeable manner no matter what the circumstances, because of his unusual composure. He went quietly about his work, and sometimes composed his poetry in low tones. My mother was quite short in stature, somewhat stout as I remember her first, with light-coloured eyebrows and lashes. She was rather more excitable, but easy-going, and she moved quickly. A more selfless person would be difficult to find. She greatly enjoyed instrumental music and song, had a pleasant voice and was very knowledgeable and always humming tunes while she worked.

My parents and their parents on both sides moved from Iceland in 1873 to Wisconsin in the USA. They were married there in 1878 where two sons, Baldur and Gudmundur, were born. In 1880 they moved to the Gardar District in

North Dakota and became settlers there. All the relatives moved with them including both parents of my mother and father, along with Jon, my maternal uncle, and Sigurlaug Einara, my paternal aunt. There were no other siblings. Their family's homestead land was near the village of Gardar, close to the land of my Afi [grandfather] Jon, where his descendants live to this day. It was there that my brothers Jakob and Jon were born. My brother Jon and Afi Gudmundur died and were buried there.

In the early spring of 1889 several families in the Icelandic community in North Dakota pulled up stakes again to become settlers in Canada. The trip was to take them to the province of Alberta, the second province from the west coast in this vast land. My parents went in that group with my three brothers, Amma Gudbjorg and Sigurlaug, my father's sister, and her family. Their destination was Calgary and since it was the last stop on the railway at the time, everyone got out there. My parents had come with all their household goods and a team of oxen. The promised land was still a long way off so it was necessary to keep going forward, travelling with heavily laden wagons pulled by cattle. The women and children remained for a time in Calgary. My mother and paternal aunt made good use of their time by working as laundresses for the so-called "gentlewomen" of the town. My father and several men from his district equipped themselves to travel on and set off with their ox team to explore the countryside. It was decided to travel in a northerly direction for some 80 miles, where the town of Innisfail now stands, and then turn west. The majestic Rocky Mountains were always visible to the west, standing almost like guardians. The mountains likely played a role in determining the direction the explorers took by luring them on westward. They crossed the swift-flowing Red Deer River, and continued onward, past fertile agricultural land until they reached the banks of the Medicine River. There they found a place to settle on amidst high hills. They selected a site for a house which has remained to this day on a hill to the east of the river. The Rocky Mountains loomed in the west more than 100 miles away and the countryside could have reminded them of their distant fatherland, Iceland. They had now travelled over 1,000 miles from the town of Gardar and there was much work to do, building homes and getting down to the business of settling on the land.

Many people may ask, "Why did they leave the fertile land of the Red River Valley and what was there to attract them to this wilderness?" There could have been many reasons. The unsettled land tempted them and encouraged them to set up shelter there and provide for themselves. There was no lack of the steadfastness, vigour or daring which was needed. I remember that my mother declared that each new settlement made them younger. Nevertheless, it must have been painful to leave her aged parents whom she never saw again, and certainly my father must have missed the many firm friends that he left behind. Those bonds of friendship were never completely severed, as evidenced by the correspondence that continued between my father and his friends all their lives. Perhaps in this isolation my father was able to find himself and devote himself more to his interests. One thing is certain, by broadening his horizons he came under influences which have been reflected in the poems that we now enjoy. Certainly the ever-changing landscape in Alberta reminded him of Iceland. He states in his poem West to the New Settlement: "After I set off to roam, I feel I have come home," etc.

Later that summer my father returned to Calgary to get the family. Nothing is said of the trip until they come to the Red Deer River. The wagon was heavily laden with household goods and my mother and three brothers sat on the top. My father walked ahead of the oxen and led them across the river. The Red Deer River often floods due to snow melt in the summer heat and is swift with a strong current as the stream comes down from the Rocky Mountains. When father led the oxen to the middle of the river the current was so strong that he momentarily lost his footing. He looked over his shoulder and my mother smiled at him and he then regained his balance. They reached the shore without further incident. In the poem Forgotten Travelling Obstacles this incident in their life was immortalized in the last two verses of the poem:

> "His wife looked at him then
> trusting with a smile on her lips
> between the children, on the edge of the seat
> Since then he always believed
> that her smile in particular was all
> that triumph depended on,
> that kept everything afloat."

I remember my mother said, "I was never afraid then," notwithstanding that in later years she was often apprehensive if her loved ones were delayed for some reason.

Then my family moved into the new home, a log cabin, and then on a wonderful fall day, October 6, [1889], my twin sisters were born. They were like night and day, the older one was dark haired and named Stephany Gudbjorg; the other one was blond and was named Jony Sigurbjorg. In the year 1893, a son was born named Gestur Cecil, in honour of the poet Gestur Palsson and Cecelia the midwife. Finally in 1900, I, the last-born baby of the family, was born and named Siglaug Rosa. My father thought that the "ur" in the name Sigurlaug was unnecessary, so I am sure that I am the only woman to have that name. My second name was my great-grandmother's name.

Later that summer my father's sister had moved with her family to the north of the District, and settled near our home, but on the other side of the river. My Amma came with her, and she moved to my parent's home where she lived until she died. Before I proceed further I would like to say a few words about them. My father's sister Sigurlaug, or "Tanta" as we called her – a term from the Norwegian District in Wisconsin – was different in appearance from my father. She had brown eyes, with smooth black hair which was never out of place. She was intelligent, entertaining and extremely calm, a true heroine in all of life's tribulations. I was never aware that she had any poetic gifts. She worked as a midwife for most of her life. She and my father did not visit each other much, though they lived so close. It was enough for them to know they were nearby. Both were homebodies and not given to travel. My greatest joy was to visit my namesake Tanta the midwife.

My Amma had two rooms for her use. There she sat with her fine handiwork and read books. Sometimes my sisters read aloud for her, because she taught them Icelandic. It was my bad luck to be the youngest and miss out on many such good things. She read English, which of course she taught herself, crocheted the finest lace, and spun and knitted with great skill for as long as she remained in good health. She also braided sedge and made hats for the boys out of hemp. She had a deep love for her only son. He had been born with a caul on his head, whether that superstition meant anything or not. My mother did her best to see that Amma was comfortable and she lived to a ripe old age. My father then wrote a poem which goes:

> *"In thanks, with its shining wreath of love*
> *here rests your weary mothering heart."*

The first years of pioneering must have been hard and busy. For two summers my father went to work as a surveyor in the northern part of the province with a group of men. I think that the "outlaw" life agreed with him. I heard him mention that. My mother remained at home with her children and Amma. One summer when my father was away a prairie fire came roaring out of the west. The fire jumped across the river and headed straight for our house. The people in the house were prepared to flee, but at the foot of the hill the soil was wet which killed the fire and everything was saved.

The first schoolhouse in the District was built on the hill just east of our house. In 1893 the men in the District built it from logs. It was named "Hola School" and the name still remains in that District. In order that as many children as possible could attend the school, those who lived quite a distance away stayed at my parent's home. Our home also became an obvious place for the teacher to live as it was so close to the school, and many of them stayed there. The school was used as a meeting hall and served as the centre of social life in the District. There were many good times had at our farm. The first Icelandic Day celebrations were held on the land there and the Icelandic flag was hoisted on a high hill northeast of the homesite. The hill has been known as "flag hill" since then. I never heard my father call his farm by name but the hills were given names: "Langas" (Long Ridge) was the ridge east of the farm and below that was "Mosamyri" (Mossy Mooreland). North of that was "Fagrabrekka" (Beautiful Slope) or "Fagrihvoll" (Beautiful Hill) and from there was a view far and wide. My father nicknamed the Medicine River "Huld" (Secret). The Indians had named it for their greatest magician, "The Medicine Man". I do not know if any magic power was concealed in its calm meanderings but it must have charmed my father, for he wrote in his poem The River: "T'would be a joy to live beside you ever and unending"– and so it came to pass.

As circumstances permitted, the house was improved and enlarged, until it took on its present form, which is how I first remember it. Most of it was built of logs and clad inside and out. First there was the hall or "Big House" as it was always called. It was a large room and had an upstairs. My father's study was west of that with bay windows facing south and two facing west. It was always called the "Kompa" (cubbyhole). In the north part of the house there was a small room partitioned off which was my parent's bedroom. Then there was a kitchen in the east part of the main house and a pantry just off it. We girls slept in the bedroom which was on the south side. The boys slept upstairs and our grandmother had the use of two rooms on the north side of the house. On the south side there was an attic, while the door on the big house faced south, with a balcony over it. This is what our home was like. We always felt it was a warm and comfortable fortress against the storms of life.

My mother was always first to rise in the morning and always brought my father and all the members of the household coffee in bed. My brothers and sisters helped with the household chores and were not often away from home. My father looked after the animals and was a true animal-lover. He worked at haying and cutting grain, especially stacking the bales. He never ground the wheat, as my mother and sisters did that. In the winter my father wrote letters and other correspondence in the mornings and in the afternoon he would go straight to his study to read and write and compose. Each moment was put to good use. I remember well on winter nights sitting in a corner in the twilight listening to him reciting his poems. In the middle of the room was a large, round fireplace which burned brightly. I remember often seeing him coming in from the barn in the cold weather, in a great hurry to write down some lines before they were lost. When my father was preparing his poems for printing, he was extremely busy and often stayed awake well into the night. Then my mother would get up at midnight and make him some coffee.

There is one unforgettable event that took place in my younger years. My father felt strongly that the school was deficient, that all students were cast in the same mould there and individualism stifled. "Here is an unhealthy atmosphere," he stated in his poem Children's School. But it turned out that I was sent to school. I was rather timid and did not know a word of English. My father took me by the hand and led me to the school and entrusted me to the care of the school teacher. I will never forget that walk. I was filled with confidence as he guided me down the path by the river.

We often had visitors. Neighbours who lived along the riverbank made it a habit to come by and chat for a while and have a cup of coffee, and they often brought the mail from town. Everyone knew how important it was for my father to get his mail. I remember my father calling, "Start making coffee, Helga, your Gudmundur has arrived."

The very first years we were there we had two visitors from Winnipeg, B. L. Baldwinson and another guest. Our house was very small, so a canvas tent was put over a wagon box and they slept there that night. It was summertime and that was quite acceptable. When the visitors were getting ready to leave, Baldwin asked "What do I owe you for the favour?" and my mother replied: "Oh bless you, don't mention it, you had nothing but porridge". He then replied "Do you think that I want to eat up all your porridge, woman!" My mother laughed at that incident.

It sometimes happened that people stayed with my parents if their circumstances were temporarily difficult. I remember hearing that in North Dakota the mother of electrical engineer Hjortur Thordarson stayed with them one winter. She was a widow with two young sons and life was tough for them. She had only one cow and made thick soup by adding grain to the milk and cooking it. Hjortur was considered introverted and dreamy, my mother said. One day, when he was near my mother's stove, one of the lids on it broke. Hjortur was so upset that my father said to him, "Oh bless you, don't be sorry about this. Maybe you can make up to Helga for the broken lid some time." Many years later he richly rewarded them. He sent my father a large collection of books and gifts of money to both of them. I said that he was making up for the broken lid.

There are many happy memories of the many travellers who visited my father, among them several ministers and professors, some straight from Iceland. My father relished becoming acquainted with them and many discussions were held on everything from philosophy to the newest farming methods.

+ poetry

Sveinbjorn Sveinbjornsson the composer came twice, and it was most enjoyable to watch him compose a tune to my father's poem "Hugsad Heim" (Home Thoughts) on our old organ. He was like a bird on a branch, the old man, as he flew from the organ to the table to write down the notes. Our mother's brother Jon, whom we always called "Unkel," came three times from North Dakota to visit us. The Rev. Rognvaldur Petursson came often. I remember that the first time that both he and his wife came the "Stampede" was being held at Benalto and my father wanted them to see that activity so much that he went with them for the first and only time. There was a heavy rainfall and I recall the trip being much more uncomfortable than it had promised to be, when we were going home.

My father was hardly ever away from home. In the early years it was customary to have community parties at holiday times like Christmas and New Year's Day. All the family would attend and stay all night. Sometimes we went east over the hill for quite a distance, as far as 10 or 12 miles. One time my father went home on foot early in the morning ahead of the other people to heat the house and feed the animals. Sometimes friends came over with the intention that "we will have a feast" and they did not come empty-handed. Generally these were "Audna-Bjarni" (Bjarni from the Wilderness), "Strandar Jon" (Jon from Geiteyjarstrond), "Vidimyrar Siggi" (Siggi from Vidimyri), Kristinn (brother-in-law) and others who joined the group. Then Icelandic songs were sung with gusto until the first rosy rays of dawn appeared. My father was no singer, but if he had a few under his belt, he would begin by singing the English hymn "In the Sweet Bye and Bye".

There were often intense disputes about the First World War. I remember that my father said that there would never be peace in Europe until all the countries would unite in the "United Nations of Europe", with a common government, and in fact many people are now of this opinion. My father was always liberal in his ideas, and his liberal views grew stronger as he aged. He had such faith in mankind that in the course of time it would be possible to educate the common people so that they could live in peace and harmony and everyone would have all they needed, provided the system under which people lived

Reputed "socialist"

26

was just. At other times there were arguments about religion. I remember that one of his old friends was rather hard on Catholic views. My father was explaining their side. In all discussions I felt he was a "Champion of the Underdog". I heard him say of the spiritualists that "This is something that we still do not understand, but maybe, when it is possible to assert that 'thoughts are things' we can understand it better".

My mother enjoyed telling us this story of the Dakota years. It was a matter of course for everyone in the United States to attend the 4th of July celebrations. The whole family went by ox team, and on one occasion when they neared a stream on the way the oxen took control away from Grandpa, waded into the water and upset the wagon, and everyone's best clothes were soaked. Someone had forgotten to water the oxen that morning. They did not let this stop them but went instead to a friend's house, dried their clothes and continued on as if nothing had happened.

When my father was able to use his study and things were quieter, and he had help with the farm, he wrote more poetry. By then he had travelled widely and come under a wide range of influences. He kept this all in his mind as he was endowed with an exceptional memory of everything he had read or seen. It may have helped that he had not attended school. Often, when something came up that we did not understand, the call went out: "Let's ask Pabbi," and he solved our problems quickly and well. Even today, when I have a problem, I ask Pabbi. I find the solutions and comfort in his poems.

If my mother was downhearted, my father used to tell her "Don't let it get to you. It will all turn out somehow." But it was in times of trouble that my parents showed their greatest strength of character. It was a tragic blow for the household when my brother Gestur was struck by lightning. Those were sad days but my father, with his usual steadfastness, had a friend build a casket for him and then he wrote a eulogy in Gestur's memory which was read at the funeral. The whole family agreed with him when he wrote:

> "Among the angelic host in joy and gladness
> Gestur will be my guest – and nowhere else. "

At the instigation of his many friends, my father sometimes travelled on long trips which gave him much pleasure and added variety to his life. In 1908 his first long trip took him east to Manitoba, North Dakota and Minnesota, and he read selections from his poetry. In the winter of 1913 he went to the Pacific Coast. He went twice to the Icelandic celebrations in Wynyard, *Sask* and the second time in 1914 my mother accompanied him. She went east to Winnipeg and North Dakota in 1911. Then there was the memorable trip to Iceland in 1917, which rejuvenated him both physically and mentally. In 1926 his friends came and took him to Winnipeg for medical consultations. Dr. Palsson came for him and my father and I travelled home together in August of that year.

Life did not seem to be so rushed in the olden days as it is now. While there were the cattle and the hay to work at, there was not as much steady work during the summer. In the first war years everyone began ploughing their land and planting grain, thus changing the nature of farm work. Our home was on my grandmother's homestead property. My father took land northeast of it which was totally hayland. Later when he got a little money he bought land beside the river and south of the home. And all that did was to add to their cares and difficulties late in life. People were starting to clear land for growing crops then. As the years passed, my father's health began to fail. My mother remained a healthy person. It was in early December 1926 and we were both at home when my father felt faint. I barely reached him in time to keep him from falling. The doctor said he had suffered a stroke but it was so mild that he did not lose consciousness. Many things were on his mind that he felt he had to finish. He had promised to compose the poetry for a cantata, and he still had some work left on Thidrandi and more things. His right hand was weak, so I tried to write for him and he finished that which he was most anxious to do. By spring he was able to walk a bit, with help at first, and later could manage to get around with a cane but he was an altogether different man, both in mind and body. On Sunday, August 9, 1927 Thorstina Jackson showed some Icelandic pictures in the old house and several older people from the district attended. The next day an unexpected telegram arrived with the news that one of my father's best friends, Jakob Norman, was coming to visit from Wynyard, Saskatchewan. They only spent a short time together that evening, for while my mother and I were doing the outside chores, we were called in and told that my father had suffered a stroke. The doctor was called, but it was to no avail, as he died a few hours later, in the arms of his friend so to speak. He had been granted his wish as he wrote in his poem Vid Verkalok (At Close of Day):

> *"And offer the world at last my reconciling hand*
> *– when the sun sets."*

When Jakob was asked why he had chosen to come at that time and had arrived on that very day, he replied he had dreamt a dream which he interpreted as meaning that he should hurry if he wished to see his friend alive.

A long time before that, my father had ordered a casket from an Icelander who was a carpenter in the district. He wanted a casket similar to the one that had been made for my brother Gestur. The grave was lined with concrete and put in order as well as possible, and so he was laid to rest in the yard (cemetery), as mentioned in one poem: "and it is a short way over to the yard." It is on the family plot on the other side of the river on his sister's land, right on the bank of the "Secret River," as he would have chosen. My mother stayed on in her home with our brother Jakob. She died in 1940 at the ripe old age of 81. She came to visit me, took sick and died from her illness just a few days later. She had been exceedingly healthy and devoted her strength until her last days to providing for her family and home. A year before she died she had the misfortune to fall and break her hip. I have always felt this verse was so appropriate for her:

> *"All life will be open, while mind and hand*
> *and heart are able to work,*
> *and the grave is sweet for a fearless soul*
> *and it is good to return to one's own."*

We humbly bless your memory, our parents, and give thanks for all your care and company on life's way. To you, my father, for the inheritance of noble ideals which you have left to us. And to you, my mother, for the warmth which you gave to our home, and your energy which enabled our father to achieve great works.

"I have long had the opinion that in other circumstances or other times my mother would have been a career student. She loved school and college." Stephan V. Benediktson

A gathering in front of Hola School, ca. 1910
Provincial Archives of Alberta, A.4669

Hola School
75th Anniversary Celebration
Rosa - 1979

Mr. President and Friends;

It is indeed a pleasure and a privilege to be present here at Hola on this 75th Anniversary Celebration.

I thought perhaps it might be of interest to review the history of the school, a bit. The first Hola School was built on my father's land, just east of the old home. It was of log construction and its dimensions were 18 feet by 26 feet, with a small anteroom. Thor Gudmundson and my father were chosen to be a delegation to legalize the formation of a school district and to see to the erection of the school. Logs were cut and floated down the river and hauled to the building site. Everyone helped with the building, which was completed and ready in the fall of 1892.

John Gudmundson was the first teacher and his only qualification was that he had himself been to school for a short period of time. There were 30 pupils and he was able to help his pupils, greatly. Other teachers followed, all from Eastern Canada. The school filled a great need in the district and the pupils came from quite distant points to attend the school. Quite a number stayed with my parents for a period of time. The school operated for 12 years. It was also the centre of all social life in the district.

Then in 1904 this present school was built and, I believe, Asmunder Christianson was the head carpenter at that operation.

Hola comes from the word meaning hilly. In Northern Iceland there is an Agricultural School named Holar and it has been in operation for a very long time. It is out in the country in a beautiful setting. There is also a church there as it is an ancient diocese and also a high tower with a stairway inside. This tower was built as a memorial to bishop Jon Arason, who lost his life during the great religious reformation which took place in Iceland in the mid 1500's. There are also other buildings such as the home of the principal and dormitories. It was my good fortune to spend one week there in 1953.

Hola has nostalgic memories for those of us whose lot it was to attend it. For myself, I had enjoyed everyday of my school life from the time my father took me by the hand and put me in the care of my first teacher, a Miss Daly, a big Irish woman who came from Eastern Canada. I remember her talking and explaining my lessons to me but I only understood two words in English, they were yes and no. But she was a good teacher and we children soon learned to understand the English language. Then a new world opened up before us.

I have such pleasant memories of my teachers, each one different but all contributing some thing of value to my life. My school mates also were a fine bunch of companions. We played hard, studied hard and always got along well at Hola.

So it is a pleasure to see how well the old school is preserved as a community centre and I wish for you and your community, many anniversaries in the future.

Thanks.

My Diary
Rosa - 1916

**Rosa as a teenager
in front of the family home**

January 1st

Well this is leap year. Pretty frosty and cold outside. Trying to snow all day. Julius stayed over night. Fan, Jen & Jake went to Patriotic Xmas tree last night. Nothing important happened. Had Plum Pudding for dinner. Jake & Julius went up to see the fellow with only one hand. Mundi came to-night. Frost came too to get his mail. they are talking & smoking in pa's room. Jake & Julius came home at about eight o'clock. He treated us on candy, gum & nuts. They had their supper & Julius ate half a doughnut, some skin of the meat, pickles on bread & a spoonful of sauce. Ma slept with me & we went to bed at $1/2$ past ten. Mundi had gone home but the rest of them stayed up all night.

January 2nd

This is Sunday & there has never been so much frost this winter as to-day. We got up late as we could not sleep well last night. The men went to bed about five. We blew the horn & sang & waked Jake and Juley. Siggi & Olson came here at two & had coffee. Jake and Juley were just getting up then. I wrote a letter to Sigrun. After dinner Fan & Jen went to Baldurs walking. Came back just after ma & I were through milking. Told us the news that a baby girl was born at Joe Hillman's last Wednesday. Julius talked & talked until half past nine when we went to bed. nothing unusual happened to-day.

January 3rd

Got up earlier than usual today because papa & Jake went to Sam Johnson's to nominate Olson. Weather the same as usual. Pa got Julius to stay here to do the chores. Jennie went to help him water the colts. Baldur went to Markerville with the cream. Mr. Hunford came back with him & they both had coffee. Pa & Jake went to M'ville & brought the mail. Mr. & Mrs. Johnson are both sick with La Grippe. Fan & Jen went over to the Johnson's to-night. nothing else has happened.

January 4th

It is cold & windy. Jake went to Olson's & John came back with him. Julius has talked & talked all the livelong day. There was to be a socialist speech at M'ville to-night & I guess they would have gone only it was too cold. I am reading Anne Karenina now. It is a good book. I took my skates off my shoes as I guess we won't skate any more.

January 5th

This is Wednesday and Julius is here yet. I'm dead sick of his gibbering. Bina & Steve are sick. Mamma phoned up to Baldur's early this morning to see how the kids were. In the afternoon ma and Jenny went to Baldur's. Bubbi came with some papers. Jake drove Julius up to Johannson's where I guess he'll stay a week or two. Ma came back alone & papa went to meet her. I guess these are the most important things that have happened to-day.

January 6th

The weather is fine. everything is the same. I'll be glad when school starts & I can get back to my studies. Fanny is ironing the washing now, at two o'clock. Jake went to Baldur's to get some hay. We are out of bread so we had (flat bread) for dinner. Pretty good! I am kind of glad that Julius is gone. He borrowed my book, 'Red Cloud'. Jenny came back with Jake. "Bibliu" Sigurdur is back again. He came to our place & Jake bought a bible. Siggi drove him to Christinnson's. There was a school-meeting here to-night. Both Arni & Gudmundur came walking. It is cold and frosty to-night.

January 7th

Cold wind, from the south. Everything same as ever. Jonas Hunford came this afternoon. Jake went to M'ville, to a Woodmen Meeting, Fanny & I gave the rest a little concert before we went to bed. Then we read for a while & so off to Dreamland.

January 8th

This is a very cold day & one likes to stay by the fire. Jake came home sometime in the night. Mr. Christinnson came for the mail this morning. There was a school-meeting & Palson was re-elected. John Hunford came to ask the girls to go to the card party with them. They said "yes" so he got them at about seven o'clock. Jake gave me the bible that he bought. I got a letter from Lillian & I sure was glad.

January 9th

This is Sunday & its terribly cold. The wind just freezes one. No one came to-day. Fanny & Jenny came home about 1 o'cl. Jenny got the first prize which was a Chocolate Box. We went to church to hear the nonsense that man said. Had coffeee at Mundi's & got home at 11. Had coffee & went to bed.

January 10th

Started school to-day with Ida Thompson as teacher. Everything went all right. There were six at school. It was terribly cold, 28° at Markerville. Coldest it has been this year. Jake went to M for mail. Came back with a new coat. Barney stopped for a second as he was going home. Frost came for mail, talked a while, then went home. Everybody talks about the cold. Nothing else has happened except Baldur went with cream to M. and we had 11 pounds.

January 11th

A terrible cold last night, 52° below. You freeze to death pretty nearly in the kitchen. more kids at school to-day. nobody came to our place. Jake has the La Grippe. Jennie went to Lilly's & swept when she came back.

January 12th

Little better weather. The sun shone brightly all day long. There was a school meeting at our place to-day & Palson came to the school for a little while. Baldur came riding to-day. He was hunting for horses.

January 13th

Pretty cold this morning. Everything the same. I got my birthday present last night. It was a ring with my birthstone in it. There were 11 at school to-day. This is all that happened to-day that I remember.

January14th

This is Friday. Same kind of weather & everything the same. Joe & Marion weren't at school to-day. Marion has the La Grippe. Jake went to M'ville for mail. Frost came over to get theirs. Papa gave me 35¢ to buy a book that Crista & I have to get. I got a pen & pen nibs from Markerville. The pen is purple. I am reading Huckleberry Finn. I read a chapter in the bible & then I went to bed. John Hunford went to M'ville & Jake talked to him a little when he was going home.

January 15th

This is Saturday. pretty cold. Ma went to auntie's to-day. Jake went to Baldur's to help him get a cow that can't stand up into the barn. Arney came to-day. He cut pa's hair & stayed the night. I am getting the Grippe.

January 16th

I got the grippe now & am feeling bummy. Didn't get up till noon. There was a band practice over at Christinnson's. Fanny & Jenny went with Arni up to Baldurs. Siggi came to band practise & stayed here till about ten. Arney went home after they came from Baldurs.

January 17th

I didn't go to school to-day & stayed in bed till noon. I'm feeling kind of tough now too. Fanny washed to-day. This is the Monday you are to give to the Patriotic Fund. Jake gave about seven bus.[bushels] of wheat & Baldur 11 bus.[bushels] of oats. Baldur went to M'ville with the cream & Jake went off to get the mail. Frost came over. Teacher came & stayed for quite a long while. Had coffee & talked for a while. Jennie has the Grippe. There was not Tatler in the News Telegram. The weather is lovely.

January 18th

I was going to school this morning but felt so bummy that I didn't go till in the afternoon. The weather is just lovely. Jennie has been in bed all day. Lalli came to-night. He was just a little tipsy. He stayed all night. The Farewell dance for Laura & Begga is to be to-night. Jake went down. Siggi stopped in on the way down. Jake got a ride with him. Lalli was here talking to us and pa.

January 19th

Now Jennie is up & Fanny is getting the Grippe. Jake & Lalli weren't up when I went to school. L. didn't go till quite a while after I got home. The dance was a success. They got up a collection for the girls. Christa was there as usual. Jake went for the mail over to Johnson's and didn't come home till we were in bed. Now they have the Grippe.

January 20th

Everything same. Weather good. Fanny is sick but not in bed. Ma went to the school house to sweep it. Jennie is over at Sam Einarson's because the Mrs is sick. Jake drove her over. Arni went past just now & I waved to him.

January 21st

Jennie hasn't come home yet. Nothing unusual happened. Awful cold. Windy & then lots of frost too to help a bit. Nobody came to-day. Don't remember how many were at school to-day. Nothing has happened that I remember except one of O. Thompson's children died just lately. It was paralysed & got the Grippe and died. I don't know what day it died.

January 22nd

This is Friday & there are only six children at school. It is frightfully cold. The wind is so sharp. Jennie is still at Einarson's. Nobody has visited us. Fanny is feeling kind of bummy.

Saturday January 23rd

Terrible wind from the south & lots of frost too. This weather is a fright for man & beast. Mamma's knee is bothering her. Fanny had a headache. I'm allright. Had a foot bath last night before going to bed. I sleep with Fanny now as Jennie isn't at home. I'm reading Robert Elsemere now. I found it in the cupboard. I like it.

Sunday January 24th

There is a band practise to-day. The weather is awful to-day. Arni came to-day. He was going to Baldur's but stayed the night. Siggi came too. There was no band practise, I just bummed around to-day as usual.

Rosa's brothers Mundi and Jake played with the Markerville Band.
Here they are shown playing for Jennie's wedding to Siggi Sigurdson, 1922.

Rosa learned to crochet during this period. She made this corset cover several years later, ca. 1925, using a pattern taken from a needle-craft paper.
Provincial Museum of Alberta, PH 73.19.99

January 25th

Went to school to-day. Crista wasn't there. She's got a cold. I was the only girl. There were six boys. Baldur came to-day & was fixing up some horse of his. Arni went with the cream & brought the mail. He took the cat home as Baldur is going to keep it. I'm glad of it. There was a school meeting here to-day. Teacher came to sign her papers. Jennie came home to-day. Sam brought her. He was half crazy. It's awful cold to-day. Lena sent us some slater [spelled slatur, it likely refers to blood sausages][8]. That's all. Now I'm off to bed after having struggled with some algebra.

January 26th

Pretty beastly cold. Teacher is staying the night here as it's too cold for her to go home. Crista was at school to-day. So were the Milne's. It was 30 below. Nobody has been here.

January 27th

I brought home Michah Clarke & am going to read it & see what it is like. Crista is reading Ivanhoe & I'm going to read it after her. T [Teacher] has just gone home. Jennie went to Johnsons. Got a ride with Arni over & is going to sweep the school house.

January 26th [this second entry was crossed out]

The weather is not too bad to-day. There aren't many at school to-day. May is sick so she doesn't come. I took home Michah Clarke & was going to read it but it was so dry that I quit & returned it. Teacher went

January 28th

Awful cold, 56 below. T. [Teacher] was afraid she had froze but she hadn't. I was alone with the boys a long time before anybody else came. Crista and Rueben were tardy. There were eight at school. I returned Micah Clarke because it is so dry & am going to take The Woman In White to-morrow. Teacher went home tonight.

January 29th

This is Friday. Little better weather than yesterday. Uneventful day. Read some of Woman in White outloud to Ma, F & J [Fanny and Jake]. Jake went to M'ville. That's all.

January 30th

January is drawing to a close. Windy to-day & frightfully dirty weather. It's hard on the cattle & horses. Nobody has come to-day. Fanny & Jake went over for the mail. The rest of us stayed home & Jennie & I read the book by turns. After putting on a clean shirt, washing my feet & putting my hair on top. I hop into bed.

[This entry had no date heading and was partially crossed out]

This is Sunday. The same infernal wind but no frost just zero. I haven't been out of doors. No one has come & we have been reading the book lots to-day. Jake has been looking after the horses etc., & pa looking after the cattle. I knitted quite a bit to-day & am getting onto the way of it. I wonder if there will be school tomorrow? Perhaps Teacher will not come if it's cold.

January 31th [partially crossed out and the date is off by one day]

Last day of January. There was school to-day as usual. The weather is good to-day & there's kind of a thaw. Teacher was sick. She might not come tomorrow if she's as bad as she was to-day. I sent for a drawing book & a pr. of hose for the 50¢ I had left. Baldur came to-day & Jake took the cream down & waited for the mail. Goodby January.

[This entry had no date heading and was partially crossed out]

1 day of February Dawns clear. I sincerely hope it won't be so cold this month as Jan. was. Teacher is sick her brother phoned us all up so there's no school to-day. Mamma's little black calf is so sick I sincerely hope he won't die. Urt our cow is getting "burtharleg"[looking pregnant][9]. Baldur came tonight

riding. We got some raw linseed oil for the calf & ma, Jake & Baldur made him swallow it. I've done some algebra. The girls scrubbed the schoolhouse floor. We are all the time reading the book. I've got a ringworm & I put some nicotine[?] on it.

Feb 2nd

No school to-day either. Lots of holidays. Calf still sick. Fan [Fanny] got a cold. Ma went to Chr... [Cristinnson's?] with a letter. Jake got mail. I did algebra & am knitting a pair of mitts for myself, if they aint too small. Nobody came. No news.

Feb 3rd

No school to-day. Fine weather. Pretty frosty last night. Everything the same. Calf sick & cow too. Aunty Lillie & the kids came to-day, so did Baldur.

Feb 4th

No school as usual. Siggi came then jake, Baldur & he went to M'ville on a Woodmen's meeting. We made Valentine's last night. Cow & calf just the same. Jake lost the mail tonight. I am knitting the mitts. We finished the book to-day & were glad it was getting tiresome.

Feb 5th

Nice weather all the time now. Got a letter from Lillian & Jennie one from Helgi. Raised the calf but he's just the same. No one has come. I'm thro with one mitt & have started the other. Jake went to Baldurs. Came back with hay load. G. Bjornson brought our mail. Arni came & Jake, F & J [Fanny & Jennie] went down to card party with him.

Feb 6th

This is Sunday & the weather's not too bad. F & J [Fanny & Jennie] went walking to Baldur's & Siggi came back with them. Jake & he went down to the schoolhouse to attend a Band Practise. Cow & calf just same. Pa went over to Christinnson's. I'm through with the other mitt pretty nearly. I s'pose there'll be school tomorrow.

[The entry for February 7th was completely crossed out]

Feb 8th

Good weather like yesterday. Mundi came while I was at school. Everything same. Crocheting tonight. I'm thro with my mitts. Read 19 pages of Ivanhoe, did Algebra & so off to bed to sleep with Teacher.

Feb 9th

Weather not too bad this morning but windy tonight. T [Teacher] is here yet. Everything same. They raised the calf & he seemed better. Just now at 15 past 11 Siggi came in a covered buggy. I got my parcel. The paints are not too bad for the price. Read Ivanhoe & did algebra & so to bed.

Feb 10th

Nothing unusual happened. Pretty cold though not as bad as yesterday. That's all. T [Teacher] is here yet & Baldur came today.

Feb 11th

Kind of chilly, but not too bad. Teacher went home with Jake when he went to M'ville for mail. the girls went to Sam Einarsons & I milked as they weren't home in time. I'm reading Ivanhoe & T. [Teacher] left a doily that she was helping me to crochet so I did a little of it. Then I washed my mitts so now they are ready.

Feb 12th

Calf is sick yet but does not have his head in the same position as before. weather has been getting better all day & is best tonight. There has been a slight breeze. Ranka and Arni Palson came. They went out for a drive & stopped on way back. I've got that ringworm or whatever it is yet.

Feb 13th

Sunday. Fanny put my hair in two curls last night. Weather just beautiful. Finished my Valentines. Made 14 in all & Jennie helped with some. Oh! the weather is lovely. The girls went for a walk. Nobody came. Jake and Jennie & I went over to Christinnson's tonight.

Feb 14th

St. Valentines Day. We'll mail our valentines in the box at school. The weather is just lovely. I got 10 Valentines. Fanny washed today. Jennie went to M'ville with Baldur & Jake & came back with Sam Einarson. Frost came tonight. The calf stood up alone for the first time. This is all.

Feb 15th

Oh the weather is lovely. There was no frost tonight & it just goes slush, splash every time to step your foot down. The girls called me when I was going home from school & I went over to Chri---[Christinnson's] because Ma & F & J. [Fanny & Jennie] were there.

Feb 16th

Lovely weather today. Snowing is going rapidly. girls went to Baldur's with Jake. John Sveinson & Gvendur Bjornson are here now. I ironed my blue skirt. We had a lesson on crocheting at school today.

Feb 17th

A Tiny bit colder today. Things all going on same way. The Masquerade is tomorrow. I won't go as usual. Gee! I wish I could go though. Nobody came & no news.

Feb 18th

This is Friday & weather is nearly the same. There was a little more frost last night. We painted a little of our flags at school today. The Masquerade is tonight. The girls & Jake went & Sellie went with F&A [Fanny & Arni] & Jake with J &S [Jennie & Siggi]. I couldn't go as soon when I get a little older I'll go when I please. I painted my flag, read Ivanhoe & went to bed.

Feb 19th

The sun shines at my window & there is a slight breeze. But weather is lovely. Bjorn Thorlackson & Jonas Hunford came tonight. We went to Bjornson's and Olsons & came home in the evening. Jake went over & got mail & brought Bjornson's and Hunfords too.

Feb 20th

Sunday. Calf died today. Poor thing. Laura came today & stayed all day. There was a band practise & we all went down & then Laura went home with Hillmans.

Feb 21st

Went to school. Weather is lovely as usual. Jennie went to M'ville with cream. A Mr. Hanson, who likes T [Teacher] brought her to school today. Mr & Mrs S. Einarson & Lillie came too. She went down to M'ville with Jennie.

Feb 22nd

Weather just the same. Nothing unusual has happened. I'm still reading Ivanhoe & crocheting roses.

Feb 23rd

Jake & Baldur went to Innisfail & Arni came here this morning. Sun shines but it is kind of cold this morning as it's windy. But better during latter part of day. They are sawing the wood down at school. We had crocheting. I've got five

roses made & am going to make a tie. We all got h'dfs [handkerchiefs?] from
Ina or Fan. & Jen. J & I [Fanny & Jennie, Jake & I] .

Feb 24th

They came home late. Weather is allright. Everything same. No news.

Feb 25th

This is Friday. Weather is nice. All Baldur's family & Lillie, & her kids & Aunty
came to say goodbye to Jennie who is going to Olds. We had drawing at School.
Baldur found Rhodystone [a horse]dead just a little east of here & she had been
dead some time.

Feb 26th

Snowed today. We went & had supper & coffee at Aunties. Jen. Fan. & I . Arni
came & went to Baldurs. They were going to Innisfail tomorrow but won't go
till monday. Jake went to Innisfail, came back at eight.

Feb 27th

The weather is fine today just a little wind. Siggi, Arni, Mrs.Hunford & John
came & were for coffee & supper. T--[?] Christinnson came tonight. This is all.

Feb 28th

Jennie went this morning. It is windy & snowing. Baldur's kids came
for $1/2$ today. John came here to help Jake. He & Arni stayed all night.

Feb 29th

Pretty beastly cold. John is here. Siggi, Baldur, Jake & he went to M'ville to
attend a Socialist Meeting. They were fanning grain. I'm reading Jane Eyre.
Goodbye February.

March 1st

Everything same. It's rather cold but the sun shone some during the afternoon. Fan. went to M'ville with Lillie & brought our mail.

March 2nd

Weather the same. We got a new calf. It belongs to mother. John is here yet. Baldur's kids go to school. Baldur came today. I'm crocheting a doily.

March 3rd

Had drawing at school. It is colder now. Everything same. Kids went home.

March 4th

Not very cold. Same.

March 5th

Asta Joharnn and Kid came also Bjorn, Siggi, Mundi Silruy & some other old guy. John went home last night. Baldur's kids came today & he came too.

Rosa's diary ends here. Her children Iris and Stephan believe there may have been more that has been lost.

"Rosa loved horses and always had horses until she left the farm. When World War II broke out she loaned two lovely thoroughbreds, Rob Roy and Black Beauty, to the Fifteenth Light Horse Brigade in Calgary to use in their training exercises." Stephan V. Benediktson

"Father's Horses Major & Charlie"

Our Horses
Rosa - no date

Rompin was a small dun gray coloured pony with a white blaze. He was very small in stature and it was said that it was because he lost his mother at birth and was raised on cow's milk. I had visions of riding Rompin when I got older but he died in 1909 quite suddenly, so there ended my dream of a saddle horse. He was bought from a man named Rompin.

Then there was Maude, a dapple-gray mare, which my brother bought. She had been brought up on cow's milk, also, she had lost her mother at birth. She was quite a good sized mare and as she grew older she became quite white in colour, losing her dapples. Talk about a cranky, cross bit of horse flesh she was the worst. She would bite and kick with her front feet. She did not want to have harness put on her, because that meant work. We girls had to haul the cream twice a week to the Markerville Creamery. It took two of us to put the harness on her, one stood with a raised club, while the other put the collar on, and then buckled the harness. She meant business too, it was no fake!

My oldest brother acquired a stallion who was called Charlie. He was bay in colour, black mane and tail, not a purebred, but had Percheron breeding. He was a very fine specimen and had a lovely contour. There were many fine horses from him and this was a great improvement in the horse breeding project, the result was that the horses became bigger and inherited many of the fine attributes that Charlie had. He was a good work horse too and was used in that capacity quite a bit.

Colonel was a lean and lanky bay. I think he was Tota's son. He was the nervous type and could have developed into a runaway horse, if given a chance. He was the ringleader of the group. We had to walk and run to get the horses in before we could embark on our cream hauling. We got them up to the gate and he saw his chance to sneak away on a dead gallop and the rest followed all the way to the far end of the pasture, every time. We had to do something drastic so we put a strap on his front leg with a length of chain on it. When he began to run, he stepped on it and tripped himself, but he became quite adept at throwing out his front leg so he wouldn't step on the chain. There are tricks in all trades.

Father's old team was Major and Charlie. Charlie was quiet, sweet tempered and so like his father, only smaller. Major was fine until he got fed his oats. Then he gobbled them up as fast as he could and kicked with his front feet. No one ever was injured, because we were wary of him, but he could well have caused trouble.

My cousin died in 1905 and owned a very nice mare called Grace. She was a light bay with a blaze and was a good saddle horse. My Auntie gave her to my oldest brother after my cousin's death. She gave him a couple of nice saddle horses.

Rosa's love of animals was not limited to horses.

She always had a variety of pets on the farm.

The Olds School of Agriculture

Although it was possible in the early part of the century for young women to go on to higher education, it was still not the norm. The opening of The Olds School of Agricultural (O.S.A.), in 1913, created a tremendous opportunity for Rosa. In 1912, the Government of Alberta began the construction of three agricultural schools, to be located on the existing demonstration farms in Vermillion, Claresholm, and Olds.[1] An advertisement in the 1916-17 A.S.A. (Agricultural Schools of Alberta) Magazine offered "FREE EDUCATION in Agriculture and Household Science for Young Men and Women". No entrance exam was required.[2] Initially, the Household Science program, which was open to girls sixteen and older, only ran for eight weeks during the winter, but the response to the program was so great that in its second year it was expanded to a full five months.[3]

Stephansson family lore suggests that the decision for Rosa to go to Olds in 1919, was not altogether straightforward. Stephan G. had always been an adamant believer in education and had been instrumental in the establishment of both the Tindastoll and Hola schools. At home he had created an intellectual environment in which to raise his children. In principle, he had no objection to Rosa attending the school; he did feel, however, that it would be unfair for Rosa to go when her other siblings had not had that luxury. There was no cost for the actual courses, but housing, books, and supplies were an issue. Helga won out and sent Rosa to Olds, paying for all of the expenses herself.[4]

In the winter of 1918-19, the year before Rosa began her program, the schools at Olds, Vermillion, and Claresholm had been closed down and used as hospitals during the devastating influenza epidemic, with staff helping to care for the sick.[5] In the fall of 1919, classes resumed and Rosa began her two years of study. The *Alberta Provincial Schools of Agriculture Calendar for 1920-21* describes the program and the courses she would have taken.

"The aim of the Department of Household Science is to train the young women of the Province to be practical home-makers. The course covers a period of two sessions of five months each. While the work of both sessions is conducted on distinctly practical lines aiming to secure the economic management of the home, the work of the first year is specially devoted to home problems and to the interests of those who have only one year to spare. The work of the second year is designed, in addition to the home-maker's course, to assist those who are preparing to be teachers in domestic science." [6]

Home Economics
Course of Study [7]

First Year

1. Cooking
2. Foods
3. Physiology and Anatomy
4. Home Nursing
5. Sewing
6. Textiles
7. Embroidery
8. Laundry
9. Household Administration
10. Sanitation
11. English
12. Mathematics
13. Horticulture
14. Home Dairying
15. Poultry
16. Elementary Chemistry
17. Civics
18. Physical Culture [Phys. Ed.]

Second Year

1. Cooking
2. Dietetics
3. Hygiene
4. Home Nursing
5. Sewing
6. Textiles
7. Household Administration
8. Home Bookkeeping
9. English
10. Mathematics
11. Horticulture
12. Home Dairying
13. Poultry
14. Bacteriology
15. Household Chemistry
16. Physical Culture

Practical Sewing class at the Olds School of Agriculture, 1916/17
Provincial Archives of Alberta, A.11390

The course calendar also gives a list of supplies that Rosa would have been responsible for:

"*Work Dresses*—Two are needed for practical work in the kitchen and laundry. These are to be made of blue chambray (at 45¢ per yard) a sample of which may be obtained at the School....

Aprons—Three are needed for cooking. These may be made of linen, heavy lawn or cotton. They must be made before the student arrives at the school.... All aprons must be plain and of white material.

Hand Towels—Four small, white, a half a yard long, having button-hole or tape, with which to fasten to band of apron.

Pot-Holders—Two. Six-inches square, covered with dress material, bound with a bias piece of material, and having attached at one corner, three quarters of a yard of white tape with which to fasten to button or apron band.

Sewing Requisites— Each student must have a large work-bag equipped with scissors, tape line, needles, thimbles, pins.

Suits for Physical Culture—May be made at the School. The girls provide their own material.

Books—Few will be required—those necessary may be obtained at the School.

Note:— (1) The students supply their own materials for sewing class, but keep the finished articles for their own use.

(2) The students are requested to have their names worked plainly on aprons and towels." [8]

**Rosa called this photo of her cooking class
"Some would-be fudgemaker's"**

Although Rosa had done some traveling with her father, attending Olds was her first experience living away from home. She thoroughly enjoyed her time at school but must have found it difficult to be away from her family. The few letters from her mother that survive are typically concerned with Rosa's lessons, her financial situation, and her general well-being. One suggests that Rosa may have boarded with a local couple for at least part of her first term. In her second year she lived in the girls' Dormitory.

O.S.A. Dormitory, 1920

Letter from Rosa's mother Helga (December 1919?)

Sunday evening, 9:00
My Dear Rósa

Your letter arrived in good time yesterday evening. I am happy to hear that you are feeling fine. Here nothing has changed. We are tolerably healthy now. Yet Jóna has been rather sick recently, the same thing as before, she has pain around her ribs. I intended to let her go to Innisfail, and now she is recovering, I think she should still go, if it will be of any use, I will try to let Wagner examine her, I think he is in Innisfail.

Jóna is writing to you now, so I don't know what news I should tell you. There is nothing that appeals to me, now. U. F. A. [United Farmers of Alberta] are going to have a Christmas tree on the 23rd, but Rúna[?] on the 24th. You must arrive home before that time. When will you come? Do you have enough time to learn your lessons? When you work so much, I would rather pay completely for your board than you have no time to learn. Is the woman not good to you? Old Welsh said he had phoned home the first evening that you were there and asked his wife how she liked you, she answered "Fine", and whether you were any "bother" no not at all.

The man [Stephan G.?] will arrive home any time now. I sent you the accounting book, it will be sent to you tomorrow morning. It takes your letter two days to arrive at Markerville. I think that my writing will stop this nonsense. I very much look forward to when you come home. God be with you and protect you.

Your useless mamma[9]

Portions of a letter from Helga (1920?)

At home on Tuesday evening
My Dear Rósa

I thank you for the two letters later last evening. Bjarni arrived with the mail, otherwise I would have not received it before tomorrow evening.... I will likely have to go faster with this letter, because I intend to send you $30. It would have been better if you had taken it with you. It is interesting that it should need to be more expensive than last winter. Flour and meat, however, are lower than they have been, and still, that the vinnukona [female farm labourer] will be $10 more expensive than the previous one, although one ought not to think about it so much. There are seventeen of you, it will be about 50 cents for each, but there's no use in talking about it, one must scrape for oneself some way out of this. You do not likely have enough fine clothes for all these gatherings, are the girls not smartly dressed? Do you like these teachers as much as the previous ones? Try to take lessons if there is any piano you can practice on....What is your place heated with? Is this steam heat good? Hannes was telling us that it takes so long to get warm, half a day he said, before it warmed up from this steam....

Wednesday morning has arrived. Either I will go with this letter or if Gudda goes, send it with her. It is dull weather and everything is dreary, Jóna is sick as usual, it seems to me, it is the old illness, and also another one, I think. At least she was not good yesterday and has not been for the past few days. I will buy a money order from Mundi and then you don't need to bother cashing this at the bank, otherwise there will be a discount on the cheque like before, now these are $30. It will not be long until I need to send another $30 I think. Well, I'll stop now. Kobbi [Jake] went to Baldur's to help move the cowshed a little, one or two rods [5 1/2 yds.] Goodbye and be careful to dress warmly when you go out. Best wishes from your mamma.[10]

In both of these letters, Helga refers to Jóna (Jennie) being ill. In 1919 she had her appendix removed, and two years later she was sent to Rochester, to have her gall bladder removed as well. [11] The letters written by Jennie to Rosa have a slightly different tone than those of her mother's. Portions of a twelve-page Christmas letter, perhaps written the same evening as Helga's, show the sisterly affection and teasing that existed between the two girls. Unfortunately, the poem she refers to, sent by Stephan G., has been lost. Another letter, written sometime later, is much more serious in its content, informing Rosa of her father's health and local concern over a flu outbreak. Although the year of the letter is not specified, the devastation of the flu epidemic in 1919 would still be fresh in local memory in March of 1920.

Letter from Jennie (December 1919?)

> *Say Rosa I have the greatest news to tell you, last night you got the sweetest dearest little calf, only fault with it was it was dead. Katy sure played a dirty trick, she "slipped" her calf, as you know she wasn't to calf till Jan.....Say Rosa will you coax Rooney Max to give us a recitation at the Xmas Tree it will be on the 24 Dec. I know it's useless to ask you for one, but I imagine you can coax Rooney for one, you ask her and tell me what she says.....the poem enclosed is sent by Dad to you he thinks it's so nice.*
> *Well be good to yourself-*
> *love from all*
> *Jennie.*

Letter from Jennie (1920?)

> *March 2nd*

> *Dearest Sister Rosa, I will write a few lines to-night to let you know that we are all on our two 'pegs' yet, all feeling first rate or as well as we usually are. Dad isn't feeling well, hasn't been all winter. he is not able*

or should not work as hard as he has to now. He says he is going to arrange things different, as he will not be able to work much longer. He will dispose of some of his lands, or try to in some way, but he would like to see some of "his"get them. so I do not know how that will work out, I know Jake is intending to buy ¹/2 of the Qr. [quarter] out north. of course there is nothing definite about it yet, or anything....

...The Jazz Outfit was supposed to be in M'ville last night & the Methodist Ladies Aid were going to have a Pie Social, next Friday but both of these are called off for an undefinite time, scared of the Flu I expect, is the cause of its postponement.

One other letter that Rosa received from home was actually written by Rúna Plummer. She was the teacher at the Hola School, who, like several others before her, boarded with the Stephanssons. She expresses some guilt about receiving their hospitality while Rosa is away at Olds.

November 23, 1919

Are there any school marms attending the Agricultural school this year? I often feel as if I would like to be there with you. Tell me what you are taught, if you ever feel like writing to me. Please don't feel as if you must write to me. I am writing simply because I would like to be talking to you deary!!!

...Your mother brought me some coffee to bed this morning. I had to take her and kiss her. Afterwards I felt as if I had stolen same from you! You have wonderfully gifted, yet human, parents! I mean they are kind to those who need kindness, when I say human. They do not 'advertise' their kind deeds. Enough Said!

In spite of missing her family, Rosa settled in at Olds, and in fact had a good deal of fun. She was actively involved in a range of social activities, making many new friends along the way. She was a member of the Athletic Committee in her first year, and served as Vice President in her second year. [12] Luncheons and parties were often held, and as mentioned in her mother's letter, she needed "fine clothes for all these gatherings." One such party was the fancy-dress affair pictured below. In her photo album, Rosa labeled it "English Lords and Ladies."

"1920 Athletic Committee
G. Graf, W. Whiteside, M. Hughes, A. Short, R. Stephansson, S. Sheppard, F. Morris,
R. Murdock, Miss Lawson, R. M. Scott, H. C. Bellamy"
A.S.A. Magazine 1920. Photo courtesy of Olds College Alumni Association

"English Lords and Ladies"
at a costume party

Of course, Rosa did not devote all of her time at Olds to parties and fun. She had always been a good student and continued to do well in her studies. Her Christmas report card for 1919 shows marks ranging from 69% to 96%. Ironically, the low mark of 69% was for public speaking, something she excelled at in later life. By the end of that year her marks had gone up, giving her an average of 85.9%. In addition to her fine academic work, she also excelled in the practical aspects of the program. At the closing exercises in 1920 she came first in a competition "for general proficiency in dairy work", receiving The Edmonton City Dairy Prize of five dollars.[13]

Left: Rosa's 1919 Christmas Report Card

Below: A copy of her final marks, hand-written by Rosa in the spring of 1920

Olds School of Agriculture

REPORT OF

Rosa Stephanson

Year Ending *Xmas 1919*

Below 40%—Failure

AGRICULTURE
- Animal Husbandry
- Field Husbandry
- Veterinary Science
- Carpentry .... Blacksmithing
- Farm Management
- Geology .... Drawing
- Farm Machinery .... Gas Engine

HOUSEHOLD SCIENCE
- Cooking
- Sewing ... 82
- Laundry ... 80
- Household Administration ... 85
- Physiology and Anatomy
- Home Nursing
- Sanitation ... 76
- Foods ... 70 ... Canning 80
- Embroidery
- Hygiene

SUBJECTS COMMON TO BOTH
- Bacteriology
- Elementary Chemistry ... 81
- General Physics
- Botany ... 74
- English ... 77
- Mathematics ... 90
- Poultry
- Farm Dairying ... 90
- Horticulture
- Bookkeeping
- Public Speaking ... 69

Conduct ... *Good*

Progress ... *Very Good*

Total average ...

Principal Olds School of Agriculture

Exam Results.

Practical Sewing ... 96
Written Sewing ... 95
Household Administration ... 80
Textiles ... 99
Cooking ... 99
Practical Cooking ... 88
Dairy ... 85
Poultry ... 86
Bacteriology ... 71
Chemistry ... 61
Mathematics ... 81
English ... 85
Home Nursing } average
Hygiene } ... 90

Total Average = 85.9

Just after Christmas in 1921, Rosa became ill and was sent home for several weeks. Many of her classmates and even her teacher wrote to her with news of the goings-on at the school. Their kind and affectionate letters show how much Rosa was missed in her absence. Parts of a letter from first-year student Marian Kocher describe a little of dormitory life.

Letter from Marian Kocher

Olds Jan 17/21

It was really my turn to write to you yesterday, but so many of the girls wrote that I decided to wait until to-day. We are having a high old time here to-night. About ten of us gathered in the parlour after supper, the teachers being away, we made considerable noise. We composed a song for the Dormitory girls and we are going to sing it next Friday night at Lit. This is the song and it is sung to the tune of 'Your eyes have told me so'

We are a bunch of jolly girls
Who came to the town of Olds.
We came to a house that faces the south
And decided that we would stop there

And then we saw the O.S.A.
Where we would try our luck
And hope to learn by the end of the term
Something of value to us.

You see we girls. We wonderful girls.
We live in the school Dormitory
We come to the school each day as a rule
We keep you all from feeling blue

When we're not here you all shed a tear
For we are the life of the School
We are the ones with lots of fun
The girls of the Dormitory.

Rosa called this photo
"Good Pickings at O.S.A. 1921"

Marian goes on to recount a reprimand given to some of the girls by their teacher, Miss Christine McIntyre. When one sees the photo of young Miss McIntyre's kind face and reads excerpts from her own letter below, it is hard to imagine that the lecture was very stern.

> *...We first year girls got a good lecture from Miss McIntyre to-day. She told us we must never call the boys by their first names, unless we know them well. We must not chew gum, or wear canvas shoes to dances, or wear too much jewelry, there was many other things she mentioned. Oh, yes. "Never wear your hair down in curls or piled too high on your head." This whole lecture was thrown at one girl I guess you know who, but of course we all took it in.*
>
> *...Your friend Marian Kocher*

Letter from Miss Christine McIntyre

Jan. 31, 1920

> *My dear Rosa, Ever since you went away I have been meaning to write you, but somehow the days have lengthened into weeks. We think about you every day Rosa, and miss you very much. However we are looking forward to seeing you before long.*
>
> *I have just come in from dinner, which we served in the dining room of the school. Mrs. Hall was the hostess to-day and will be to-morrow. We had roast chicken, riced potatoes, creamed peas, celery, cream of tomato soup, bread and butter, cream pie and coffee. Before long our Rosa will be getting us meals in the O.S.A. dining room. Miss Clutton, Dorothy Harding, Elise Harding, have already served....Well Rosa, I must stop now, as it is getting late. We are hoping to see you back next week. Night night. Get well as soon as you can.*
>
> *Lovingly yours   Christine McIntyre*

Rosa (top left) with some of her classmates. She titled this picture "A rose among thorns" referring to the young man in the centre.

Rosa graduated from O.S.A. in the spring of 1921, returning home to live on the farm until her marriage, in 1928. Her photo albums contain dozens of pictures of the many friends she made, showing just how special that time in her life was to her. She continued to keep in contact with classmates, attending reunions well into her senior years. Later in her life, when she was able, she also made financial contributions to the Olds College Foundation.

In the 1921 *A.S.A. Magazine* [Alberta Schools of Agriculture], Rosa's graduation photo (see pg. 51) appeared with the following caption:

> ROSA STEPHANSSON: *"When she will, she will; and when she won't, she won't. And the reason why she won't is – just because."* Just because Rosa was born in Alberta we are proud of her. Just because she is Vice President of the '21 Athletic Committee it is a success. Just because we know her so well, we feel her *"because"* is always founded on thought and merriment. Just because she has – never told us what her future intentions are, we draw our own conclusions.[14]

When talking about this part of Rosa's life, one must not forget her closest friend, Hannah Johnson. Their friendship began in Markerville, but Hannah did not go with Rosa to Olds. In 1919, the same year that Rosa began her program, Hannah went instead to Normal School in Calgary, to get her teaching certificate. Their letters during this period, and the years leading up to Rosa's wedding show the strong bond that existed between the two women. Although Hannah lived and taught in several different towns, they continued to keep in touch, writing long epistles to one another. The two remained friends for their entire adult lives. The following group of letters from Hannah helps to illustrate their close relationship.

Above: Hannah as a young woman
Right: Hannah in 1952

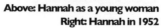

Rimby, Alta.
Mar. 16th/23

I have been writing the last part of this letter after school but I must go and wash the blackboards for Monday. I am the janitor, you know. Anything for a bit of filthy lucre!! I am so glad you like your lessons. I have been inquiring about correspondence lessons in music lately and one or two people who knew anything about them said they were very good. Oh! don't you just love your piano? I think I will try to hoard up enough to get a piano.—— I could get one by paying some down and the rest monthly. Daydreams! Daydreams! I have 3 physical Culture Mag. [magazines] I may just save them for you until I come home.

High River, Alta. Oct. 3/25

Wasn't it funny that we both should feel so blue about parting that day! Is it an omen of some kind? As for losing me, I will never never give you up no matter where you go. You are always my best friend and chum and if we are separated some day we can write to each other anyway. Let us always be dear friends as now [initials D.V.?]! What say you dear heart?

High River, Alta. Feb. 18/26

I miss you just terribly. I have no girl friends here: they are all "matrons". ahem! or else just kids that I teach (from 13 to 17).

[continued Feb. 22nd] On Saturday I got your letter, and oh boy, wasn't I glad. I have thought of you so much lately that I must have sent you a telepathic message, and hence your letter! I didn't get the first part of my letter more than started when I had to quit. I surely do enjoy your dear old newsy letters; it seems as if we are really talking together.

Three Hills, Alta. Apr. 15/28

It makes me positively homesick, because it's about four o'clock, the usual kaffi-time [coffee-time]. What would I not give to be with you and your mother and Jake, this lovely Sun. afternoon. I guess she's washing the coffee pot or something!

....I hope I can see you this summer anyway. Hurry up and get married so I can come to visit you! I won't for centuries, if ever, so don't worry about me anymore. Bye bye honey. This letter is an unearthly length. now be sure to write immediately. With oodles of love to you & the folks. As always, Hannah

This letter from Hannah was written in response to the news of Rosa's marriage to Siggi Benediktson, June 17, 1928.

Three Hills, Alberta
June 23/28

My Dearest Pal and Friend,

I want to wish you every joy and happiness that can be thought of in your new life work. Your letter gave me so much pleasure because I could read you were very happy, my darling. I am sure Siggi must be a real fine man or you would not give yourself to him, and I hope that I, too, may know him well some day. I certainly intend to take advantage of your invitation, and no later than this summer! But there is just one thing that I am sorry about and that is this – I wanted to give you a shower, in the worst way, and now I can't.. If you had only put it off till August! but I know that your two months of happiness before then will mean more to you than a "shower", but it was for my own pleasure I wanted to do it. However, I am sending my own little contribution anyway, even if it didn't get into your hope chest.

Write and tell me what you have got for presents – but goodness gracious – you did this all so fast that you have taken our breath away and nobody's had a chance to turn around even!

....Boy oh Boy! How can I wait a month before seeing you, but there's nothing for it – I'll have to. Give S. [Siggi] my congratulations and best wishes. When I see him I'll give him some good advice learned from Dorothy Dix!!

As ever
Hannah

Raising a Family

Family and friends at the wedding shower

Rosa first met Sigurdur 'Siggi' Benediktson when he visited the Stephansson family home. She later told her children that he was very quiet but that she was taken with his blue eyes and black hair.[1] The two were married in the spring of 1928, and their first child, Helga Iris, was born one month after the stock market crash of 1929. The depression years were a challenge for the young couple; however, Rosa soon learned that her husband was not only handsome, but hard working and committed to the welfare of his family.

Sigurdur Vilberg Gudmundson [Benediktson] was born in Riverton, Manitoba, on May 14th, 1901. A year before Siggi's birth, his father Benedikt Gudmundson and his mother Ingibjorg had emigrated from Iceland with their two infant daughters, Sigurrose and Olafia (known as Loa). After their arrival in Canada, Siggi, his brother Karl, and sister Margaret were born. Sadly, in 1905, Sigurrose and Margaret both succumbed to scarlet fever.[2] The last child, Leo, was born in 1906. Only two years later, the family faced another great tragedy when Siggi's mother Ingibjorg passed away.[3]

Rosa and Siggi after the wedding

Unable to both work and care for his children, Benedikt sent the two youngest, Karl and Leo, to live with relatives. In 1911, Siggi's great uncle and namesake, Sigurdur (Sam) Benediktson, asked that Siggi be sent to live with him in Alberta. Siggi arrived in the Heckla district accompanied by his older sister Loa. Sam and his wife Vilborg's first son, Emil Benedikt, had died as a child in Iceland. They later adopted another son, Skuli, but he contracted tuberculosis and passed away when he was only eighteen.[4] The Benediktsons eventually adopted Siggi as well, but Loa, who was two years older, was not adopted. Sam and Vilborg also opened their home to a motherless neighbor girl named Margaret Bjornson who lived with them for several years.[5] Loa lived with the Benediktsons for three years before joining her father, Benedikt, and his new wife, Gudrun, in Prince Rupert. Benedikt and Gudrun had two sons of their own, Rurek Reimar (Ray) and John. [6]

Right: Siggi and Loa

Below: Siggi (far right) at his confirmation, ca. 1914
Provincial Museum of Alberta, PH75.28.5

After the Gudmundson family left Prince Rupert, Loa returned to the Benediktsons' where she remained for nine years until her marriage to farmer and WWI veteran Haldor (Dori) Johannson.[7] Siggi's brothers, Karl and Leo, also moved to Alberta. Karl settled on a farm near Edmonton, and Leo did some ranching and owned hotels in Wildwood and Grimshaw before becoming involved in the oil business.[8] Although Siggi had now become a part of the Benediktson family, he also took time to see the Gudmundson family. In the 1920s, Siggi, his birth father, brothers, and half brother, made several trips up North to fish, taking horses and sleighs out onto the lakes. [9]

Leo and Siggi horsing around while on a fishing trip

Like many of the women in the Stephansson family, Siggi's adoptive mother Vilborg was an active member, and for a time, the president of the Icelandic Ladies' Aid Society, called Vonin or 'Hope'.[10] The values of service to community were passed down to Siggi, who was later to serve on the Heckla School Board. As a young man, Siggi took it upon himself to raise money to purchase some land in Markerville for a community park. He drove a democrat (buggy) around the area asking for donations for the project. Later, ball diamonds and a curling rink were built, and the annual Icelandic Picnic has been held there for many years.[11] In 1950, the park was renamed Stephan G. Stephansson Memorial Park, and a cairn was erected in the poet's memory.

Siggi's adoptive mother, Vilborg (center)

Sam and Vilborg Benediktson were a generous couple, willing to open their home to Siggi, Loa, and Margaret. Siggi learned a great deal from his adoptive parents. He may have inherited his athletic ability from his birth parents, but his love of literature and passion for chess came directly from Sam. Siggi was only twenty-four years old when Sam passed away, and four short years later, in 1928, Vilborg also died. That same year, on June 17th, Siggi married Rosa Stephansson and took over his parents' farm. [12]

Right: The Benediktson home, 1926

Below: Iris and Stephan

The young couple struggled through the 1930s and added two more children to their family. Stephan Vilberg was born in 1933, followed by Conrad Benedikt Jon in 1937. Farming was difficult, and Siggi resorted to a variety of methods to support his young family. He bought a truck and hauled grain, cattle, gravel, and even crude oil. He also tried his hand at selling Esso products from the farm, and buying cattle for commissions agents, Adams, Wood and Wyler.[13] Rosa of course was busy caring for the three children as well as working on the farm. Although they were happy years, it was not easy.

Siggi hauling grain to Innisfail

Rosa and Siggi had been married for twelve years when, in December of 1940, Rosa's mother Helga passed away at eighty-one years of age. She had deteriorated after suffering a broken hip.[14] The loss of her always strong and supportive mother was a great blow to Rosa, and in her grief, she was utterly unprepared for the shock that was to follow. Helga was buried in the Christinnson Cemetery, and the family gathered at the Stephansson home after the funeral. Rosa's sister Fanny, who was fifty-one, had come with her husband, Arni Bardal, and their son, Gestur. While returning to Baldur's home that evening, Gestur, who was driving, strayed from the road and the car rolled over. Fanny was killed.[15]

Helga, Rosa, and Iris

A young Fanny (left) with her twin sister, Jennie

Somehow the family managed to carry on despite their tremendous loss. Time passed, and in June of 1942 Rosa gave birth to thier last child, Sigurdur Theodor Oliver. The new baby brought some joy back into their lives and for a while things were looking up. However, supporting the growing family remained a challenge. Even though they had managed through the depression, WWII had begun, and farming was still a difficult way of life.

In an effort to stay out of debt, Siggi made the decision to sell his parents' homestead in 1942. He bought a bare quarter section east of the Tindastoll School. In his memoirs, Stephan V. recalls that in the fall of 1942 "...my father, with the help of my bachelor cousin, Steve Stephansson, a good carpenter, built a 24 by 30 foot shell of a building to live in on the otherwise bare land. Father said it would become a chicken coop after he built my mother's dream house on the hill. The view of the Rocky Mountains from that hill has been imprinted in my mind for life."[16]

Siggi on his horse 'Bill'

The family's dream was shattered only weeks later,
on November 14th, 1942.

S.V. (Siggi) Benediktson, well known resident of the Markerville district died suddenly while enroute to town on Saturday. He had been ill for several days and started for town to see his doctor. He drove as far as the Stockel farm and stopped there to see if someone would do the driving for the rest of the distance. He collapsed while at the Stockel farm and died instantly. Cause of death was a ruptured aorta of the heart.[17]

Rosa never really got over the death of her husband. The series of tragedies that she had to endure were heartbreaking, and suddenly she was left with four children to support. Teddy was only five months old when his father died. Apart from the practical concerns of life, Rosa was still grieving. She never remarried and always remained faithful to Siggi's memory. Her son Stephan remembers that period well. "One of the saddest sounds stored in my memory are the sounds of my mother dancing alone at night to the music of the Oldtimers on the radio in that lonesome house on the prairies."[18]

Although Rosa had spent her life living and working on a farm, running it was another matter. Stephan recalled that "Mother was not very mechanical and not very confident when driving a car. Being the youngest of a large family, she had not developed many business skills either."[19] The next few years were very difficult, but Rosa managed to raise her children and keep the farm going.

Rosa with her Studebaker, 1952

Iris, Stephan, Conrad, and Ted

Gradually the family adjusted to their new life. Rosa worked on the farm, the children went to school, and, like any other family, the normal daily routine took over. Rosa's lifelong habit of clipping articles continued and she carefully saved anything that she thought might be useful. She kept up this practice for the rest of her life. Along with household hints, she also saved recipes, poems, song lyrics, and articles, ranging in subject from world events to cats.

Valentines from Con and Ted

Like most mothers, Rosa also saved many things associated with her children, such as cards, certificates, and news clippings. She was always very proud of her children and their accomplishments. The two valentines shown above were lovingly hand drawn by Con and Ted. Con's card reads "Roses are Red, Violets are blue, Mother[s] are wonderful and especially you". Ted's simply says "For my heart, from Teddy".

Teddy and his bike

As the children grew, they were gradually able to take more responsibility on the farm. In 1947, Iris, who had just turned eighteen, married Alfred William Bourne. The Bournes had a farm only about four miles from the Benediktsons. The older boys, Stephan and Con, began to do much more of the farm work and helped their mother greatly. For several summers, during haying season, Rosa left the boys to go and help her brother Jake at the Stephansson homestead. She would do the cooking and milk the cows while the men brought in the hay. Alfred would drop by periodically to check on the boys.[20]

Iris's eldest daughter, Marie, born in 1948, was only six and a half years younger than her uncle Ted. She recalled hearing about one incident when the boys were raking and the horses decided to run. Con was thrown forward and landed in the basket of the rake. The rake bounced along and was finally tripped, dumping Con out safely. Miraculously, he walked away with only a few scrapes and bruises. Not wanting to worry their mother, the boys kept the incident to themselves, even when she asked why they were so roughed up. They made some excuse about wrestling and she reprimanded them for fooling around instead of working.[21]

Con also escaped serious injury when, in 1949, the brooder stove exploded. He was rushed to the hospital with burns, and fortunately, he fully recovered. In a strange coincidence, the *Red Deer Advocate* article reporting Con's accident was printed right next to the announcement of his uncle Baldur's death.[22] Baldur was sixty-nine years old. Mundi had passed away two years before, when he was sixty-five.

As the eldest son, Stephen felt a great responsibility to help support his family. He finished school in Tindastoll in 1947, and began attending the new Red Deer Composite High School, but took several weeks off that first year to work on a threshing outfit. In an effort to improve the family's financial situation, he would take on a variety of jobs each summer while continuing to work on the farm. In 1951, Stephan added a year to his age to obtain a chauffeur's license, so that he could work as a trucker.[23] The following winter, because he had the license, Stephan was offered a job at a sawmill near Whitehorse. Although Rosa wanted him to continue school, Stephan felt he needed to work. At seventeen, he left school and hitchhiked to the Yukon, returning in the spring to help out on the farm.[24] In 1953, Stephan began his career in the oil industry when he got a job as a roughneck.

Rosa and Conrad

About this time, Conrad also left the farm to begin working. He was only fifteen when, in 1952, he moved to Red Deer to apprentice as a sheetmetal worker. He then went on to S.A.I.T. (the Southern Alberta Institute of Technology) in Calgary, to get his Journeyman papers. Settling in Edmonton for a time, Con worked for the Westeel Corporation on a number of construction projects.[25] Stephan recalls that his younger brother "loved the construction business, but more particularly heavy equipment: trucks and earth-moving equipment. As a child Conrad would spend hours pretending to drive a big truck."[26]

Stephan landed a job with Imperial Oil in January of 1955, working on a drilling crew. The new job not only had better hours and employee benefits, but also higher pay.[27] He was able to build a house in Red Deer, and Rosa and Ted finally left the farm and went to live with him there.[28] By now Ted was thirteen and nearly ready to start attending High School. Living in town, and with her farm work behind her, Rosa was also able to think about making changes in her life. It was only a year or so after arriving in Red Deer that she got a job as a Nurse's Aide at the Red Deer Hospital. The steady income, job satisfaction, and social connections from her work added greatly to her life. She thrived at her job and was eventually put in charge of a surgical unit.[29]

In the spring of 1956 Stephan was on his way North to work in Norman Wells. At the airport in Edmonton he met a young woman named Audrey Jones. Audrey was also on her way to work at the camp, running the "Rec Club".[30] Over the summer the two saw alot of each other, and they were married in Calgary that December. The following year, after returning to Red Deer, the couple's first son was born. Rosa was, of course, working at the hospital and was a great support. Many of her grandchildren and even great grandchildren were born at the Red Deer Hospital, and Rosa made sure that they and their mothers had the best possible care.

Stephan graduated from the University of Alberta in 1962

Three months after the baby was born, Stephan decided to return to high school.[31] Soon afterward, he enrolled at the University of Alberta in Civil Engineering. In order to pay for his education, Stephan had to sell the house in Red Deer that he and Audrey had been sharing with his mother and brother. Rosa and Ted found an apartment, and Stephan and Audrey left for Edmonton.[32]

Rosa was very proud of her children, and in keeping with family tradition, she encouraged them in their educational pursuits. In a letter to Stephan in 1959, Rosa gave him a full account of Con's marks, as well as congratulating him on his own.

Sunday Afternoon

Dear Stephan, –

Thank you for your letter. It acted like a shot in the arm as an antidote for butterflies in the tummy.

Cons marks came this wk. It seems your marks tally about the same. Congratulations on your hard earned success. Civil E [Engineering] & Math lead well above average.

[con't]

Here is Con's story.

Attendance	*Possible 228 hrs.*
	Actual 210 "
School Rating	*71%*
App. Board Rating	*74%*
Practical	*73%*
Employers Rating	*75%*

School Remarks:
Willing, cooperative, capable, steady worker.
Awarded 4th year technical credit.
On receipt of $3 fee, Apprenticeship Certificate will be issued.

Pretty good isn't it! I am very happy for you both.
Everything here the same. Ted is tootin his flute in preparation for more lessons.

The same letter picks up a few days later. Con had returned to Red Deer and was preparing to marry Linda Schultz of Bashaw in August. Rosa writes about plans to purchase a house with Con and Linda. Although she seemed somewhat apprehensive, they did move in together, along with Ted. A year later however, Con and Linda moved to the Yukon, where Con first worked as a sheet metal worker, and then landed a job in charge of maintenance for a section of the Alaska Highway. Rosa bought the house, which was only a few blocks from the hospital, and remained there until she moved into a seniors' apartment many years later.

....Well, I guess the house situation is being put through and I hope it is for the best Con wants to go halves on it with me. I did not suggest it, but it ought to be a good enough deal, if we both cooperate. It will be a strictly business deal and we will put everything on paper. I pay the down payment & then he pays the rent till he has paid $1595 & then $1/2$ each. Linda and him have of course discussed it and I have told him to consider it well from every angle.

....I have deposited the down payment & Spud says the deal should go through. This house can be sold anytime we hope, if the bottom doesn't fall out of everything if we so desire. A Muttart home and a basement suite would of course have cost less & paid for itself, but that is out of the question now....

While Ted was still living in the house with his mother, he was apprenticing as a plumber/pipefitter in Red Deer. He completed his studies at N.A.I.T. (the Northern Alberta Institute of Technology) in Edmonton in 1963, becoming a journeyman plumber/pipefitter. After getting his papers, Ted went on to work for Lockerby and Hole, construction contractors in Edmonton. He worked on many large projects in Edmonton, the Northwest Territories, and Saskatchewan. He later owned and operated a service station and car wash in Grande Prairie.[33]

Ted at the piano

Of the three boys, Ted was the one who most resembled his father. Rosa mentioned in her letter that Ted played the flute, and, as shown in the previous photo, his musical talents did not end there. He was also interested in drag racing and skidoos, and became a senior member of his Masonic Lodge in Edmonton.[34] In 1965, when things were becoming serious with his girlfriend, Ruth Metcalf, Con wrote the following letter lightheartedly warning him of the perils of marriage. Ted was not put off by Con's teasing, and he married Ruth in 1966.

....How's the car working & how's this girl friend we here so much about. Is there any bells in the air or is it not come to that yet. Marriage is a wonderful thing if your not the nervise type. You have to have fast reflexes and eyes in the back of the head. Every now and then when the saucers & rolling pins are flying, the kids crying because there hungry & got wet pants & suppers burning on the stove & the cat just knocked over all the plants, the canary gets loose, it sure is nice to have a nice quiet job to go to with only bulldozers & trucks with no mufflers running around. But really its not that bad. I wouldn't change it for a million dollars....

**Back: Ted, Audrey, Con, and Linda
Front: Alfred, Iris, Ruth, Stephan, and Rosa**

Rosa's children were now grown and she was in her sixties. She was finally ready to give up working full time and pursue other interests. Although her official retirement was in 1968, some family members recall her still having some involvement with the hospital well into the 1970s.[35] Even after her retirement, Rosa kept very busy, devoting more time to preserving her father's legacy. She began recording family history and acting as the family spokeswoman at many Icelandic gatherings. She also had more time to travel and visit her growing family.

"Bennie's" retirement party, 1968

Once Iris's five children were of school age, she too decided to take on some new challenges. In typical fashion, Rosa saved clippings of Iris's graduation and work as a real estate agent. In 1972, Iris began working for Swift Realty in Red Deer, and for a time in 1974/75 she had her own company, DD Real Estate.[36] Eventually, the demands of the farm became too great and she left the business.

**A clipping of Iris (top right)
when she was a real estate agent**

Rosa's grown children continued to work and expand their own families. The last of her twelve grandchildren was born in 1974, and she also had several great grandchildren by then. Iris and Alfred had five children: Marie, Margo, Bill, Tom, and Jim; Stephan and Audrey had three: Steve, Susan, and Paul; Con and Linda had a girl and boy: Darryce and Darryl; and Ted and Ruth had two sons: Ted and Derek. Rosa's family was always the centre of her life. She had devoted herself to the difficult task of raising her four children alone and, as she got older, she was able to enjoy fully the family that she and Siggi had created.

Rosa and her family, 1975

Contribution to Community

Rosa was raised with a strong sense of community. Her pioneering parents had been instrumental in the development of several social institutions in the Markerville area, and they had instilled in Rosa the need to be actively involved. Her father had helped to establish several essential services for the local settlers, including the Post Office and the Markerville Creamery. He also pushed for the intellectual betterment of the community through the building of the Hola and Tindastoll schools, the creation of a debating society, and the formation of a library.

The Gardar Ladies' Aid,
North Dakota, late1880's

Rosa's mother, Helga, had been an active member of the Gardar Ladies' Aid, in North Dakota. This society, established in 1885, was organized to raise money for a variety of community projects. A new society, called Vonin, or "Hope", was created in Calgary, ca. 1891, with Rosa's aunt Sigurlaug serving as its first president. The group was then transplanted to the Markerville area, where it is still serving the community. Rosa's mother-in-law, Vilborg Benediktson, was also a member, and she too served as the President for a time.

Rosa joined Vonin in 1928, the year of her marriage, and remained active in the organization for the next fifty-one years. The Stephansson and Benediktson family traditions carried on when Rosa's daughter Iris joined in 1948, shortly after her own marriage. Iris's daughter Marie also eventually became a member.

For many years, Rosa served as the Vonin secretary. Until 1977, the secretary recorded the minutes for all of the meetings in Icelandic. Since many of the younger women were no longer fluent in the language of their mothers, it was decided that the society minutes should be taken in English. Rosa continued as secretary for two years after that, finally retiring from the group in 1979.

In 1973, Rosa submitted an article about Vonin to the Spruce View Historical Society's publication, *Grub-axe to Grain*.[1] In it she gives a brief history of the society and describes some of their activities. Following her article is a copy of the Vonin Regulations. They were hand-written by Rosa in English in 1976, at the front of the minute book.

Vonin Ladies' Aid
Markerville, 1960's
Rosa (far left)
Iris (third from left)

Markerville Icelandic Ladies' Aid (Vonin)
Rosa - 1973

In 1888-89, groups of Icelandic families arrived in Calgary, most came from North Dakota. Their idea was to settle in the area west of the Red Deer River. Calgary was the terminus of the railway and the homesteads were one hundred miles north west of the city. It was a point where the Icelanders could get ready for their pilgrimage into the wilderness. The men went ahead, leaving their families in Calgary, while they found places for them to live.

It was during this time that the women joined together and formed the Ladies' Aid. No doubt they felt the need of social contact and could accomplish more by organizing. By 1895 most of the group had dispersed to the new settlement.

They called this: Ladies' Aid "Vonin" which means "Hope". First president was Mrs. S. Christinnson [Rosa's aunt Sigurlaug], Mrs. H. Goodman was chosen Secretary and Mrs. C. Bardal, Treasurer. A code of rules was drawn up, which incidentally have been adhered to, in general principles to this day. Basically the chief aims were: 1. To help the ailing and the needy. 2. To support efforts for the religious education of young people. 3. To give support to the church particularly the Lutheran.

In June 1912 there were twenty members. There are now nine active members. Freda Olson, President; Lilyan Johannson, Treasurer; Rosa Benediktson, Secretary. It is unique that the minutes are still being written in Icelandic, and that this organization is still active after more than eighty years in operation. In order to raise funds for their charitable work and enterprizes, two social functions were held. It could be a Box, Pie or Shadow Social, or Cake Cutting contest. Twice, cards were sent out with a small bag attached and a little verse requesting that for admission fee you put in as many cents as the years you had lived.

In the fall there was a Tombola, or Bazaar. Members sewed and contributed articles as did non-members. A person received a free draw with the admission. Extra draws were 25 cents. This was very popular, especially with the young people.

The aid did their share in contributing to the social needs of the community. First in the old log school at Hola, later in the Fensala Hall Markerville. The meetings at members homes were enjoyed by everyone involved, there were many pleasant memories of these occasions. There was an Icelandic Celebration in the form of a picnic every year and the Ladies' Aid always had charge of the refreshment booth. Every function wound up with a rollicking dance. In later years when members were less active, their funds were raised by raffles.

The upkeep of the Lutheran Church was of concern to members. They instituted the Cemetery Clean-up Day, which bore good results. A gate for the Cemetery and signs for the Hall and Church have been erected for posterity. In all their undertakings the Ladies' Aid (Vonin) have had wonderful support and co-operation from the community, without which their labour would have been in vain.

We would like to think that the small rays of "Hope" which we have been able to give to humanity along life's highway, have been inspired by that small group of courageous women in Calgary and for this and all other blessings we are sincerely grateful.

Rosa at a special meeting of Vonin, November 20, 1979

Four generations attended, including her daughter Iris, granddaughter Marie Chaumont, (beside Rosa), and great granddaughter Tara

After 51 years, Rosa left the society

Vonin Regulations [2]

I. This Icelandic Ladies'Aid shall be named "Vonin" hope.

II. The aid shall be independant from other organizations and unbiased in word and deed.

III. Its Aims and objectives are:
      (1) To foster and strive to educate young people in Christian faith
      (2) To aim at helping the poverty stricken and those ill and suffering hardships
      (3) To support the Christian Church and especially the Lutheran

IV. The Officers shall comprise:
      A President, Secretary and Treasurer chosen at the annual meeting

V. The President calls the meeting to order and presides over it.
The Secretary writes up minutes of the meetings and other secretarial duties
The Treasurer looks after the financial duties

VI. The fees to be .50¢ per annum for new members, and .25¢ there after

VII. No member younger than 15 years admitted.

VIII. Annual meeting to be held October 15th, or as close to that date as possible, every year. The treasurer reprt to be audited.

IX. If a member desires to resign from the organization she expresses her wish at a genereal meeting, or she may send a written request, providing she does not owe any fees.

X. If one half of the members are present, a meeting may be called.

XI. In presenting motions at the meetings, the majority rules when voting.

As Rosa grew older, her social role evolved. Although she was not one of the first settlers in the area, she was certainly an early member of the community. Her knowledge of local history and her position as the daughter of Stephan G. made her a sought-after spokeswoman. More and more, she was invited to speak at a variety of functions and to serve as a representative of both her family and her community. One speech, given in Red Deer in 1981 for the Status of Women Day, is "Pioneer Women", a tribute to those women who endured the hardships of homesteading in Alberta. Rosa herself was honored as a pioneer in 1980. Red Deer M.L.A. Norm Magee wrote the following letter of thanks.

October 18th, 1980

Dear Mrs. Benediktson,

It was indeed a pleasure for me to present to you a gold medallion on behalf of the Government of Alberta.

Please accept this coloured photograph of you receiving the medallion as a gift to you on behalf of the Red Deer 75th Anniversary Committee and myself.

May I once again extend to you a hearty congratulation on receiving this gold medallion. It is but a small token of the appreciation that the people of this community and I, wish to extend to you for your help in pioneering this great province.

Best of luck to you always.

Yours sincerely,
Norm Magee,
Member of the Legislative Assembly

Pioneer Women
Rosa - 1981

Madam chairwoman, Ladies and Gentlemen;

The role of the pioneer woman was different from the present day life of a housewife. They lacked the amenities, which we of this modern age, take so much for granted. They had to be brave, fearless and resourceful, in order to meet the needs of their family, and to take part in the building of a good community, from a wilderness area.

It required strong faith, and determination to come to an unknown land, where you had to carve out your existence, with your bare hands, so to speak. I do not ever recollect hearing of how hard a task it was. Rather it was a challenge, which that hardy breed of women met with courage.

Both my grandparents with their teenage children emigrated from Iceland in 1873 to Wisconsin, U.S.A. and settled on a homestead. Their next move was to Pembina, North Dakota. Again they homesteaded in the fertile Red River Valley, in contrast to the hard wood forests of Wisconsin.

Then after sixteen years in the U.S.A. my parents decided to come to the North West Territories. So in the spring of 1889 they set forth, bound for Calgary, which was the railroad terminus at that time. The family consisted of my parents, their three young sons and my paternal grandmother. Their destination was what is now the Markerville district some ninety miles north of the city, where a group from Dakota had gone the year before. My father set out to locate a homestead and to build a home while the family stayed in the city.

In August my father returned and so began the sojourn to the homestead, which would take four or five days with a team and wagon. Crossing the Red Deer River was often a stumbling block in those days as it floods in the summer when the mountain streams which feed it, melt. My father led the horses across the river but in midstream he felt as though he was about to be swept downstream. He looked back at mother and she smiled at him and he regained his footing and all arrived safely across. Later he composed a poem in which he attributed their good luck to the encouraging smile that my mother gave him. "I was not a bit afraid" my mother told me.

On October sixth that fall my mother gave birth to twin daughters. Her next door neighbor did midwifery so she officiated and all fared well. My mother perhaps had some duties that were not common to all pioneer women. My father was a poet and in addition to being a "tiller of the soil" he devoted any time off, such as rainy bad weather days when he couldn't farm and wakeful nights to the pursuit of his hobby, as he called it. It was imperative that my mother see to it that he was not unduly disturbed when engaged in his literary work. When he was preparing his manuscripts for the publishing of his poetry he worked most of the night in order to meet the deadline for the publications. My mother would get up in the night and brew my father some coffee, which I am sure was greatly appreciated.

The first school in the community was built just east of my parents home on the homestead. Several young people stayed with my parents for a period of time in order to avail themselves of a bit of education. School teachers quite often boarded with us down through the years. The school was also the center of social activities. My mother and aunt sang in a choir which one teacher organized. He accompanied them on his flute. The Markerville Icelandic Ladies Aid Society was a pioneer venture. Established in 1891, it is still functioning. The ladies prepared the lunch and made coffee in my mother's kitchen for social functions. In appreciation they presented my mother with a silver tea service before the turn of the century.

My mother acquired a new range with a warming oven and reservoir, early, possibly the first in the community. She also brought a new sewing machine with her from the U.S.A., a gift from her father and brother. This of course was an invaluable item for the pioneer woman who had to have dress making capabilities. She was also able to help her neighbors who had no machine but several daughters.

My parents had a family of eight, six reached maturity. One son died from diphtheria in the U.S.A. and my sixteen year old brother was struck by lightning and died instantly, so they had their share of sorrow, as did most pioneer families. But they met trouble with outward composure and my father composed touching poems to their memories.

Those pioneer women often had to be alone with their young children on the homestead whilst their husbands sought employment away from home in order to acquire some cash. My father was away from home for two summers with a survey crew around Edmonton in the very early years. So my mother with her young family and my grandmother were alone on the homestead. Prairie fires were prevalent at that time and dreaded. One such fire came raging from the west fanned by a strong wind. It jumped across the river, headed for the house. The family had packed up what they could and were ready to vacate. Luckily there was a damp, boggy area just below the house so the fire died down and all were safe.

My paternal grandmother made her home with my parents. She was a frail woman, but lived to be 81 years of age. I never saw her do housework but she was an artist at turning virgin wool into wearing apparel for the family. She spun very fine wool, sometimes three ply. She knit lovely lace from sewing cotton and followed the English instructions, a language which she taught herself to read and understand. She gathered reeds, dried and braided them and made straw hats for the boys. Such resourcefulness!

My brothers made their homes with my parents for a period of time after they were married while they were building their homes. There was always plenty of company at our house. Neighbors dropping in on the way to town and of course on the way home to bring the mail. There seemed to be more time for neighborly visits then. So my mother had a large family to cook for and it required skill to do it economically and well.

Pioneer women were often called upon to administer nursing care and doctoring to their families as the closest doctor was in Calgary during those earliest years. My sisters developed a severe type of whooping cough. My parents feared for their lives. But my mother nursed them back to health. I had pneumonia when I was young so at the first sign of a cold I well remember the hot ginger tea I had to swallow, which I detested, and the hot mustard foot bathes I had to take, But it must have been the right treatment for me.

So you see those pioneer women besides being a good helpmate for their husbands had to be industrious and skillful in many facets. We gratefully acknowledge their contribution to the building up of our lovely land and the secure home life which they helped to promote for us. We revere their memory.

Thank you.

Rosa giving one of her many speeches

Rosa's many public appearances were nearly always related to her family and heritage. On more than one occasion she was asked to speak at the annual Icelandic Day Picnic, held in Markerville each June. Her speech in 1975 gave a detailed account of her return trip to Iceland the previous year. While there, she had again acted as a representative of her family, revisiting the cairn to her father that was was erected twenty-one years before. In the following speech, given at the festivities in 1976, Rosa describes the humble origins of the Icelandic Day celebration itself.

Icelandic Day
Rosa - 1976

Mr. Chairman, Guests, Friends and Old Neighbors:

I hope you don't think it presumptuous of me to reminisce a bit about Icelandic celebrations of the past. Don't misconstrue that I think I'm getting old, it's just that I have been around for a long time.

The first Icelandic celebration in this settlement took place on June 21, 1889, the second year that the settlers were here. It was held on the homestead of Sigurd Bjornson, which was just up the river from our old homestead. Everyone in the community was present. There was a program of songs and speeches. There was some discussion as to what would be an appropriate name for the new settlement. Medicine Valley was suggested but no definite decision was made. It was always referred to as the Alberta or Red Deer community.

My information comes from the pen of Jonas H. Hunford, who wrote a concise and authentic history of their community and its inhabitants which was published in Almanak, edited and published for years by Thorgeirson of Winnipeg.

August 2nd was celebrated for years as that was the day that the first declaration was made that led to Iceland's Independence. Later, June 17th was celebrated as it is in Iceland, that being the birthday of the great statesman, Jon Sigurdson, who played such an important part in the struggle to gain the independence which was finally established on December 1st, 1918.

The celebration was held on our old homestead in very early years. Hola School was there and it was the center of social activities at that time. On top of the round hill east and north of our old farm home, they erected a flag-pole and a flag was unfurled. Ever after that hill was called "Flaggholl" or Flag Knoll. The other surrounding hills were also named.

One celebration was held at our old homestead when I was only eight years [days?] old. Mother told me she had attended it for a short while. Many years ago Mrs. Christinson. John Christinson's mother, told me this story. She said, "I saw you when you were only a few days old." She said my father was very happy and said to her, "Have you been to the house to see ogn." My interpretation of ogn is "the mite". I'm glad they didn't call me Ogn. Anyway, new-born babies quite often are not things of beauty except in the eyes of the parents. and I know I was no exception.

In 1911, the celebration was held on the old Strong homestead. John Strong was my brother's [Mundi's] father-in-law. The Innisfail band had been hired to come and entertain. It had rained copiously so the roads were a quagmire and the horses had a hard time to get through with the result that the band did not arrive until after 4 o'clock. Everyone waited patiently, or impatiently, and when they arrived the show was on. To verify my statements, I have a letter, which my father wrote to my mother relating to her the events of the day. Mother was on a visit to Winnipeg and North Dakota.

For years the celebrations were held on the community picnic grounds. In approximately 1925, my late husband, Sigurder Benediktson, collected money in from the community to purchase the grounds. His ledger notes, "Subscription List for buying Picnic Grounds for the Community of Markerville," with a total of $214.60 collected from 64 donors. The grounds were held in Gili Bjornson's name until it was acquired by the Province of Alberta in 1950 and named the "Stephansson Historic Site". In the early days a platform was erected under the trees with benches for the audience. They remained there for years. Many noteworthy citizens were invited as guest speakers and the old settlers were able to express themselves quite profoundly. There were sports, a tug of war, baseball matches and a a dance in the evening.

Quite often it rained for June is generally our rainy month. One year it even hailed and I can recollect everyone rushing for shelter, but the show went on.

In 1911, there came to Markerville a Professor Sigurd Helgason with his family. He lived in the old Disher house in the hamlet. Perhaps the fact that his wife's brother, Jonas M. Johnson, owned the farm that Mac Hansen owns and the hamlet was on his land. Regretfully he was not mentioned in the district history that was recently compiled. Helgason was a musician and composer, as was his father before him. He set about to establish a choir and a band right away. The band was made up of the local farm boys from the Icelandic community. contributions of money were made to buy the instruments and they were off to a start. They practiced evenings after work and on Sunday at Hola school. Unfortunately, Helgason did not stay long in the community, but the boys did not let that deter them. They kept on and quite a few of the local boys must have been musically inclined for they led the band for years. Men, such as W.S. Johnson, Arthur Thompson and B.G. Bjornson joined. They became quite proficient for as well as providing entertainment in the district and at the celebrations, they travelled up and down the line to fairs and stampedes for years. I don't remember what year they disbanded, but in 1922 they were still going strong. I believe Fred Olson and Joe Johnson are the only members still with us. They enriched their own and our lives with their music.

Thank you for your kind attention to my ramblings.

Rosa in Icelandic costume, 1950s

**Rosa in the costume of the Fjallkona,
or "Lady of the Mountains", 1978**

Another aspect of the Icelandic Day festivities is the naming of the Fjallkona.
Each year, a woman is chosen to take on the ceremonial role of the "Lady of
the Mountains". The Fjallkona was an idea born in Iceland more than
two-hundred and fifty years ago, but it wasn't until the mid 1970s that
the Leif Eiriksson Club of Calgary, the Nordurljos Icelandic Society of Edmonton,
and the Stephan G. Stephansson Icelandic Society of Markerville began the
local tradition of naming a Fjallkona annually. The clubs alternated in chosing a
woman to represent their area, and Rosa was the first Fjallkona from Markerville.[3]
She recieved this honour at the Markerville picnic in 1978. For her acceptance
speech, Rosa chose to include the beautifully descriptive poem "In Remembrance",
which was one of Stephan G.'s most famous and often-quoted works about
his homeland. Afterwards, she was photographed in the costume of this
symbolic representation of Iceland.

Fjallkona
Acceptance Speech
Rosa - 1978

Mr. President, Members of the Icelandic Society and Friends;

This is indeed a great pleasure to me, to be present here today as a representative of our community to honor the Motherland, Iceland.

Perhaps it would be in order for me to explain a bit about the origin of the "Fjallkona" or Lady of the Mountains as it may be termed in English.

It is a symbol of Iceland, the motherland of our Icelandic ancestors. The idea was thought up by a gentleman in Iceland by the name of Eggert Olafsson, in about 1750. The white head dress symbolizes Iceland's snowy mountain peaks, and the green cape, the verdure of her lush lowland meadows and valleys.

The first ceremonial appearance of the Fjallkona took place in Manitoba in 1924, at their Icelandic Celebration, and has continued since, and the custom was taken up by other communities. Later, Iceland took up the custom, so now on their National Holiday celebrations, June 17th, the Fjallkona makes her appearance on the balcony of Government House, and greets the Nation.

The Icelandic immigrants remained devoted to their Motherland, but they came to love their Fosterland Canada, with deep and loyal affection. They came to better the lot of their descendants and themselves, and we Canadians think they chose wisely and well. They added a shining thread to the tapestry which combines the cultures and traditions of the many Ethnic groups, which go to make up this Canada of ours today.

So to commemorate their heritage, Icelandic celebrations were instituted, and became a yearly event.

The first such gathering was in Milwaukee, Wisconsin in 1874. The first gathering in this community, was in 1890, at the farm of Sigurdur Bjornson, on the banks of the Medicine River. Manitoba will be celebrating for the 89th consecutive year this summer. It will be held at Gimli, early in August, [it] is a 3 day event called the "Festival of Manitoba".

In 1904, my father composed a poem especially for the celebration here in Markerville. It must have struck a very responsive note in the hearts of various people, because that poem is often quoted, several musical composers set it to music, and there are translations of it in the English language.

[Rosa first recited the poem "Tho thu Langforull Legdir"in Icelandic]

It was translated into English by the linguist genius, the late Dr. Watson Kirkonnel. He calls it:

Remembrance

Though you have trodden in travel
All the wide tracks of the earth,
Bear yet the dreams of your bosom
Back to the land of your birth,
Kin of volcano and floe-sea!
Cousin of geyser and steep!
Daughter of downland and moorland!
Son of the reef and the deep!

High over heaven and landscape,
Haunting your thought as it strays,
Torrents and towering summits
Tremble once more to your gaze.
Far in the outermost ocean
The isle of your heart is awake,
Shining in shadowless summer,
Showered with light for your sake.

Vivid that Icelandic vision
Viewed in your dreams as they run—
Granite rocks growing with flowers,
Glaciers warm in the sun,
O kin of volcano and floe-sea,
Cousin of geyser and steep,
Daughter of downland and moorland,
Son of the reef and the deep.

As a symbol of the Mother image of Iceland, I would like to bestow my blessings on her descendants wherever they may be, and urge them to preserve and cherish their precious cultural heritage and to contribute the finest elements to our Canadian nation.

I wish to thank Shirley Lundberg, the retiring Fjallkona for having carried on this tradition so successfully, during this last year!

I wish for the Icelandic Societies continuous future successful enterprises!

I wish to thank the people at large for their attendance, which clearly indicates that they appreciate the efforts of the committee, who have successfully organized this celebration.

Lastly I would like to express my gratitude to the people who afforded me the priviledge of representing the Fjallkona here today.

Thank you

[In one of three slightly different versions of this speech, Rosa added the following comment.]

Note: to verify my statements re: dates of celebrations I would refer to the Thorgeirsson Almanak, and an article about the Fjallkona published July 20th 1967 in Logberg Heimskringla.

Stephan G. Stephansson, 1913

**Rosa overlooking
the Medicine River**

The Poet's Daughter

When Stephan G. Stephansson died on August 10th, 1927, Rosa was just twenty seven years of age and soon to be married. She had loved her father deeply and had always taken great pride in his work. Before his passing, Stephan G. had made some arrangements for the management of his literary legacy. He had named his friend Rognvaldur Petursson as his literary executor, and bequeathed the publishing rights for his poetry to the Icelandic Federation of the West.[1] However, the family also felt a great responsibility for the preservation of his work.

Soon after his death, plans were underway for a variety of publications of Stephan G.'s poetry and letters. He had always had many literary friends, and they were determined to pay tribute to the poet. Although Rosa was busy raising a family in those first few years, she gradually became more involved in the process of disseminating her father's work. She had known many of Stephan G.'s friends her whole life, and after his death Rosa began to correspond with them as her father had.

Over the years, several projects to honour the poet were undertaken, and cenotaphs were erected in the Markerville area and in Iceland. The first of these was unveiled in July 1936 at his grave site in the family cemetery, which was just across the river from the Stephansson home. His friend and neighbor, Mr. Ofiegur Sigurdson, was "the prime mover in erecting the memorial". It was "financed by popular subscriptions, the money being raised by Mr. Sigurdson's efforts among the Icelanders in Canada and the United States."[2] The *Red Deer Advocate* described the event, mentioning many of those who spoke or took part in the ceremony. Although the family was present, they did not have an active role.

Red Deer Advocate, July 22, 1936

The Cenotaph is a fitting tribute to one who was so close to the hearts of his people – a pioneer, philosopher, poet and friend. The memorial is rugged, simple, yet a beautiful piece of workmanship and a credit to the committee who conceived the plan and to the workmen who carried out the details of construction.

The second cenotaph erected was unveiled in Markerville on September 4, 1950. The Historic Sites and Monuments Board of Canada, in co-operation with the Alberta Provincial Parks Board, built the monument and officially opened the Stephan G. Stephansson Memorial Park. A local committee had also taken part in the planning of the park, including Rosa's close friend, Hannah Johnson. Stephan G.'s eldest surviving son, Jakob, unveiled the cenotaph in front of a crowd of about three hundred and fifty people.[3]

Officials at the unveiling of the Markerville Cenotaph, 1950

Jakob is third from the right
Provincial Museum of Alberta PH75.28.7

Eventually, Rosa, the youngest of the Stephansson children, began to take over the role of family representative at the many events honouring her father. She was frequently asked to speak at ceremonies and celebrations of all kinds, and she took this responsibility very seriously. In her many addresses and written accounts she recorded not only the achievements of Stephan G., but also the history of her family and community. Her speech, "My Father", given at the site of the Markerville cenotaph ca. 1981, gives a brief account of Stephan G.'s accomplishments and the honours bestowed upon him after his death.

My Father
Rosa - ca. 1981

Friends and Fellow men:

I have been asked to say a few words about my father. My father was born in Iceland on October 3, 1853 and emigrated to Wisconsin, USA with his parents in 1873. Five years later my parents were married, my mother having arrived in the USA with her parents, in the same group of emigrants. They spent 16 years in the USA and then in 1889 they came to Alberta and for the third time pioneered a wilderness area. This became their permanent home, thenceforth.

Father was a hard working farmer all his life. He was endowed with a great gift of poetic ability. He worked on the farm in the daytime, for he had a large family to support, but at night he sat up and wrote his poems which are named, "Wakeful Nights". He was entirely a self-educated man. He wrote the great volume of poetry in Icelandic but was very proficient in English and several other languages as well. Several of his poems have been translated into English and more no doubt will be done. As well, he carried on a vast correspondence and took an active part in all public endeavors during his 38 years of residence in the area. He had a staunch and loyal partner in my mother, whose untiring efforts for home and society at large were remarkable. My father passed on in 1927 and my mother in 1940. They are buried in our family cemetery across the Medicine River, near the old home.

A cenotaph, erected by family and friends was unveiled at his graveside in 1936. The Dominion of Canada Historic Sites and Monuments Board erected this cenotaph in this park at Markerville in 1950 and dedicated it on September 4 of that year. My brother Jakob, unveiled this cenotaph. This park was named the Stephan G. Stephansson Memorial Park. In 1953, Iceland erected a cenotaph near his birthplace in Northern Iceland. I had the privilege to be invited to unveil that monument to my father.

The old home was declared an Historic Site in 1975 and this last couple of years has been nearly restored to its original state. That project will be completed next year. The old home is located on the east side of the medicine river about two and one half miles from the hamlet of Markerville.

I am sure this could not have happened anywhere else but in our Canada and in our Alberta, the country my parents came to love as their own. Canada is a multi-cultural land and encourages the different ethnic groups to cultivate their cultures and literature and thus add to this tapestry which makes up our Canadian ancestry.

Thank you.

Rosa, Jennie, and Jakob beside the Cenotaph in Stephan G. Stephansson Memorial Park, Markerville, 1950

Rosa at the gates of the Christinnson Cemetery

In the spring of 1953 Rosa received an invitation from the Government of Iceland to attend the celebrations for the one hundredth anniversary of her father's birth. Rosa was delighted to be given this honour and the opportunity to travel to Iceland for the first time. She was to be present at the unveilling of a third cenotaph, on Arnarstapi, a hill near Stephan G.'s birthplace. In an effort to share some of the excitement of receiving the invitation, Rosa wrote a few paragraphs about the arrival of the mail that day. It took more than one attempt for her to compose the lines that captured these important emotions, and Rosa wrote them on a torn piece of notebook paper.

A Penny for Luck

The morning of April [?] 1953 dawned clear and sparkling as only an Alberta spring morning can be, with its promise of untold wonders about to unfold. The usual tasks on the farm awaited doing. They were the routine chores of administering to the wants and welfare of the various farm animals and lastly my three young lads. But what a red letter day in my life this proved to be ere it closed!

Living beside a rural mail route makes farm life so much richer and more rewarding. The highlight of the day was when the mail truck went by. There was always anticipation over what he might leave in that small metal box. Surprises, sometimes sadness, but always a flurry [of] excitement and if he didn't stop, the day [lost] some of its glamour.

....My young son came bouncing in with the mail shouting Special Delivery Letter for Mum. Hmph! I grunted thinking this was just a prank but no there it was as he said. I sat down & opened the letter and noted the contents that was an invitation to visit Iceland.

Rosa's first trip to Iceland was truly one of the highlights of her life. It had only been eleven years since the death of Siggi, years of farming and raising her children alone. By the time she received the invitation, Ted was already twelve. For a few weeks, Rosa was able to leave some of her responsibilities behind her and make a pilgrimage to her parents' homeland. She wrote many letters home to the family giving details of her adventures. In spite of being kept very busy while on her trip, touring the country and attending dinners and celebrations, Rosa was still able to worry about home and her young sons.

14 July [1953]

....I did not tell you about our landing in the plane at Reykjavik. We are met by crowds who line the airport. I am presented with an armful of beautiful roses by the wife of the prime minister. Then a man from the broadcasting station asks if I will say a few words to the people over the network so I had to say of course later on. We proceeded to Augusta's home where I am to stay and I take a bath etc. etc. & drink coffee & more coffee. Then this gent calls for me to do a bit on a tape recording and read 2 verses of one of Dad's poems. Then rush back to dress for dinner at the prime ministers. We go there and are well dined & wined for everyones taste.

Leaving New York for Iceland, 1953
(Rosa is at the base of the stairs in a grey suit)

July 17th
Reykjavik

Dear Boys,

Just a few lines to let you know what I am doing. Just now I am nursing a cold but my hostess just bought me some good medicine so it will have to make itself scarce very shortly. Won't be long now. Tomorrow we go on our trip north for the unveiling. Gudm. [Gudmundur] Halldorson the man of the house here is going to drive as the prime minister cannot go till that night (Sat. nite) he is so busy with his duties, but the prime ministers lady will travel with us. It takes about 6-8 hrs. to get there and everyone is hoping for good weather of course on the 19th.

I have been very busy this wk. mostly visiting museums and friends and drinking coffee and eating innumerable cakes. Been out till about 1 o'clock every nite. Reykjavik people don't sleep too much the days are so long now. The weather is very mild but most of the time the sky is grey even tho it isn't raining and one misses the bright sunshine out west.

I am sure gardens and crops are looking fine although Jennie tells me they had a bad hail storm. Pretty early for that.

Hope you are making out not too badly. How do you like batching [baching]? I s'pose by now you are used to it.

Am looking forward to setting my foot on good old Canadian soil, although this trip has been one wonderful adventure which I will appreciate more as time goes on.

[con't]

Hope Con & Theo are fine and you are able to get clean clothes. When Iris comes with the children be sure and watch that they don't play near the water tank if it's full, it should have a lid on it I guess.

Can't think of very much to write about. Next week will be very busy and I won't write much more as I will likely get there as soon as the letter. Will send one from Newfoundland tho.

Best regards and keep well & happy
Mum.

The cenotaph erected on Arnarstapi, a hill in Iceland, for the 100th anniversary of the birth of the poet

The monuments that were built in Alberta to honour Stephan G. became important destinations for many dignitaries who visited Canada from Iceland. Rosa proudly welcomed Icelandic President Asgeir Asgeirsson to the Stephansson home in 1961. Several years later, he wrote a brief letter to Rosa, recalling his visit.

Asgeir Asgeirsson
2/2 1969

Dear Rosa Stefansdottir

Thank you for the last time, when we met at your old home and at the commemorative marker of your excellent father.

It is special for a remote nation to come into possession of such an excellent poet from a foreign country. We can never be sufficiently thankful for it.

It has now been a long time since I met your father Stefan. I think it was 1917, and I am grateful for these memories of that outstanding man.

The hammer and the anvil from your home- [illegible] are still on my desk, but they will probably later go to the National Museum in memory of St. G. St., the best son, who moved abroad.

Give my thanks to Mr. Kerry Wood for the book!

Yours sincerely, Asg. Asgeir [4]

Icelandic Prime Minister Bjarni Benediktsson also visited Markerville in 1964, laying flowers at the cairn in Stephan G. Stephansson Memorial Park. In 1989, then-President Vigdis Finnbogadottir made her pilgrimage to the home and grave site of the poet, saying "I've always dreamt of coming here to see with my own eyes the landscape in which he wrote his immortal poetry. Today this dream has come true, and I'm not disappointed."[5]

All of the honours and memorials were, of course, due to Stephan G.'s masterful poetry. From the time of his death until Rosa's own passing, nearly seventy years later, she answered hundreds of requests regarding the publication, translation, and adaptation of her father's work. She corresponded with many of Stephan G.'s literary friends who worked to make his poems available to a wider audience. Rognvaldur Petursson, a close friend and the founder of The Icelandic National League of the West, had been made literary executor prior to the poet's death. In 1938 he wrote to Rosa from Winnipeg regarding the publication of a book of her father's letters. In it he also mentions that Helga was ill. Rosa's mother was seventy-nine years old at the time.

Dec. 19, 1938

My Dear Rosa,

I received your letter one and a half weeks ago, but it so happened that I unfortunately lay flat on my back. All the same, I intended to try to answer before this, but I succeeded no further than to write out a small cheque to your mother and worked continuously there. Now I have been up and about here from noon, and therefore want to shoot out these lines to you. Read this note to your mother, because it is naturally intended for you both.

I believe that when your mother first experienced this shock to need to lie down in hospital, then her need would be only a few cents, as it has been a good year with you. These dollars are straight from me, because there is nothing in the funds from publishing yet as things stand, but significant new expenses to get the publishing of the letters started. But later there will be something, if one waits long enough.

Now the first volume of the letters has arrived here, but it sits at customs, because I have not been able to find the time to do what needs to be done to get them out. All the same, they will be ready on Tuesday.

Who should I ask to sell them in your area and how many copies do you think should be sent?

We send our sincere regards to your mother and wish her a good recovery and happy holiday. I send my greetings to all your people. Goodbye.

In friendship
Rognvaldur Petursson[6]

One of the issues raised repeatedly in many letters was the quality of the poetry translations. Many attempts were made at translation, and Rosa was often cautioned to be careful in her choices for publication. A letter from Paul Bjarnason, who had translated some poems himself, strongly advised Rosa to reject inferior work.

[Vancouver, B.C.] Dec. 3 – 1965

Dear Rosa, – Your letter came yesterday and I am a bit puzzled as to what to say.

The fact that your father was the only immigrant poet that the Can. Gov't. [Canadian Government] has significantly honored with a monument should be enough for us Icelanders to want to see to it that his works are not misrepresented by ambitious, but unable translators....We cannot afford to have a masterpiece mutilated beyond recognition.

....I think that you should strive to find out through L-H. [?] who have done some translations; and then the whole output could be classified and the misfits winnowed out. I think your idea will not be too far from mine; but anyhow this is your baby and I shall never complain.

With best wishes as ever
P. Bjarnason

Finnbogi Gudmundsson, Icelandic scholar and still a family friend, made great contributions to the preservation of the legacy of Stephan G. Stephansson. He held the first Icelandic Chair at the University of Manitoba, later returning to Reykjavik where he became head of the National Library of Iceland.[7] In 1953, he arranged for artifacts to be moved from the Stephansson home to the University of Manitoba for their display and safe keeping.[8] That same year, he sent a letter to Rosa urging her to write an article about her parents. This article later became *Foreldrar minir* (My Parents), published in Reykjavik in 1956. He asks: "Have you had any time to be able to begin on the memoirs of your parents? I remember many things that you told me last summer [in Iceland] and it will have an excellent home there. Now just be energetic in getting down to it!"

Professor Gudmundsson wrote many articles and volumes about Stephan G. over the years. In an excerpt from a 1971 letter he again mentions the memoirs and asks for Rosa's permission to publish a rare letter written by Helga. Following that is another letter written in 1980. It once more addresses the issue of quality translations.

20 / 6 1971...

Dear Rosa,

....Then I would like to publish a section from one of your mother's letters to your father that was in the group of letters, and she wrote it to him while he was on a trip to Iceland in August 1917. I hope that you allow me to publish a section of this letter, and then it will first appear in the volume. How is it Rosa, do you not have any other photograph of your mother than the one you lent me that appeared in the book Foreldrar minir [My Parents], your memoirs of your parents? If you have another photograph of her and some other photographs of your father than we know of from Bref og ritgerdir [Letters and Essays], will you be sure to loan me them? I will then send them back to you immediately.

....Yours Sincerely,
Finnbogi G.[9]

The National Library of Iceland
Reykjavik, 18/10 1980

Dear Rosa,

Best thanks for your letter, dated last September 11, which reached me right before I left on a summer holiday abroad, so that I did not have the possibility of answering you before now, with arriving home.

It pleased me to hear that work has begun on rebuilding your parents' old farm and that a certain collection of English translations of your father's poems is going to be published. This, of course, is a problem because it is not enough to print everything, it is necessary for whoever takes care of the selection to select from them and then discuss a lot. It is more sensible to have the volume smaller and of good quality.

I enjoyed hearing from you who is to see about the publication and when it is expected.

[He goes on to list some translations that he has sent to Rosa]

You should be allowed to keep up with which translations will be accepted and be strong in not letting other translations be printed than those, with which you are really pleased.

It is also important that a good preface be written for the publication. I understand that an excellent Icelandic man is at the University in Edmonton, and he will take care of this, it's just like him to consult with Haraldur Bessason in Winnipeg.

Allow me to keep up with how the rebuilding of the old farm goes.

With best greetings from us here,
Yours sincerely,
Finnbogi G.[10]

The publication referred to in the letter was a volume of selected translations from Andvokur (*Wakeful Nights*), compiled by the Stephansson House Restoration Committee after the work on the house was completed. The Committee decided to print a book of poetry when it became apparent that there were sufficient funds remaining after the restoration. A substantial amount of interest had accrued from the original donations for the refurbishment of Stephansson House, and using the money for the publication of some of Stephan G.'s work seemed an appropriate choice.[11]

Many such projects were undertaken during Rosa's lifetime. She recieved dozens of letters requesting information about her father or permission to publish his work. In 1945, Mrs. Thorstina J. Walters wrote from New York, asking for information for her book on the Icelandic Communities in North Dakota. In 1972, Rosa received a letter from Paula Vermeyden, an enthusiatic teacher in Rotterdam, Holland, who studied Icelandic and was simply fascinated by the poet. In the 1980s an Edmonton musician and composer, Richard White, set several of Stephan G.'s poems to music, and playwright Dorothy Clancy included three works in one of her plays. It must have been very satisfying for Rosa to know that so many people not only took an interest in her father's poems, but that they were also passing along their knowledge and appreciation of his work.

Rosa at the Cenotaph in Markerville

Stephansson House Restoration

One of the greatest pleasures of Rosa's life was witnessing the restoration of her family home. Designated an historic site in 1976, Stephansson House was finally opened to the public in the summer of 1982. As the last surviving child of Stephan G., Rosa played an important role, providing the restoration committee with information about the history of the house. She also acted as a spokeswoman for the family, speaking at both the dedication and opening ceremonies.

Stephansson House in 1907

Within the Icelandic commmunity, discussions about the fate of the house began many years before the Government of Alberta became involved. As early as 1953, Professor Finnbogi Gudmundsson arranged for some of the contents of Stephan G.'s study to be moved to the new library at the University of Manitoba, where they were preserved and displayed for many years.[1] By 1970, the family was making inquiries to the Glenbow Archives in Calgary, seeking advice on how to preserve the house, both as part of the historic record and as an actual site. Mundi's daughter-in-law, Ellen, the wife of Jack Stephansson, wrote to Rosa to tell her about her visit to the Glenbow.

August 14, 1970

Dear Aunt Rosa,

Last monday I took the privilege of contacting the Glenbow Historical Library and Archives Dept. and told them of your father's house that still stands at Markerville. They seemed very interested and she said that she would like to send someone out to Red Deer to get more information.

....Edwin [Mundi's son, living on the neighboring property] is so unsettled he has no idea what he is going to do as yet. However if he should sell his place this will be the end of the old house as it wouldn't have any value to the buyer. The windows have been broken again so that means it's not going to remain clean for visitors.

....The two pictures of your mother and father should be taken out of the old house as they may be destroyed. The old stove and whatever else is left there, such as his chair must be saved. Wish a replica could be made, using some of the old materials. It would be placed here in Heritage Park where thousands of people could enjoy what he [Stephan G.] gave to the world. Somehow I feel if we really make an all out effort something could be done, before it's too late.

The idea of building a replica of the house in Heritage Park in Calgary never came to fruition; however, efforts to save the original house soon began in earnest. Along with the family's efforts, the Icelandic Societies in Markerville, Edmonton and Calgary began to lobby the government for support in saving the homestead. On April 4, 1972, the Icelandic Society of Edmonton wrote to the Historic Sites Branch of the Provincial Museum of Alberta voicing their concern about the future of the property. Eventually the government came to agree that the homestead was of great importance and they began the process of designating the house as an Historic Site.

Provincial Museum & Archives of Alberta
Historical Site Branch
12845-102 Avenue
Edmonton 40, Alberta

Attention: Mr. John Nicks

Dear Sir:

As Albertans of Icelandic descent, we are most anxious to see the home of author Stephan G. Stephansson in Markerville restored and maintained as an Historical Site in Alberta.

Alberta is not in a position to lay claim to very many authors, nor, for that matter, is Canada, being a very young country. Therefore, it seems a pity that something should not be done to recognize one who was an Albertan. The people of Markerville, as well as our Society, and the Icelandic Societies of Red Deer and Calgary would very much appreciate the Historical Sites Branch involvement in this project. All of the above groups are small and are not in a position financially to undertake this project. We are, however, very willing to assist by approaching the present owners of this site to ascertain if the home and sufficient property may be donated to the Historical Site Branch for restoration and maintainance by them. We would also attempt to locate and return as many items as possible, which may have been removed from the house.

Trusting you will give this matter very serious consideration, and a favorable reply may be received by us, we remain,

Yours very truly,
The Icelandic Society of Edmonton
B.A. Thorlakson, President. [2]

Although it had not yet been officially designated as an historic site, on August 10, 1975, a dedication ceremony was held at Stephansson House as part of a celebration of one hundred years of settlement in the area. The next day, the Red Deer Advocate reported that "About 1,000 people from throughout the province turned out for the event".[3]

The article went on to say that "Mrs. Rosa Benediktson of 5730 41st St. Crescent in Red Deer, youngest daughter of the poet, received a special tribute from the Icelandic National Choir. The choir gathered in a circle before her to sing one of her father's poems. 'This is a truly momentous occasion,' said Mrs. Benediktson. 'My family's dream has finally been realized', she said, thanking the Icelandic societies in Markerville, Edmonton and Calgary for their work in pressing for the restoration of the house."[4] Rosa gave a speech at the event, honouring not only her father but also remembering the women who pioneered alongside him.

Rosa speaking at the Dedication Ceremony, August 10, 1975

Bottom left: Members of the Icelandic National Choir

Dedication Day
Rosa - 1975

Master of Ceremonies, honorable guests, Eastern and Western Icelanders, Friends and Relatives:

Welcome to this, our old Hola Community. This to me is a momentous occasion. Down through the years many people have expressed the desire, that this, my parental home be made an historic site and now that dream is about to be realized. I consider myself most fortunate to have lived to see this day.

I do not know if fate decreed it thus, but by some strange coincidence, this is the day my father ended his earthly career, August 10th, 1927, 48 years ago. But my father lives on in his literary work and poetry, as long as the Icelandic language is spoken, for poetry is an integral part of their lives. This was apparent when the Icelandic immigrants came to America. No matter how poverty stricken they were they brought their precious books along. From these they gained inspiration and courage to carry on in spite of difficulties.

And as we dedicate this day and reflect on my father's life, let us think for a moment of the women who had the greatest influence on his life. We here in Canada are being reminded that this is "Women's International Year" for some reason. I do not know why.

There was my father's life companion, for their paths led together since they were very young in Iceland. I am, of course, referring to my mother [Helga]. They were married at Green Bay Wisconsin, in the United States on August 28th, 1878. She was then 19 years of age and he was 24. It must have been what we call today, a double ring ceremony for my mother had had a five-dollar gold piece made into a wedding ring for my father. She was a tower of strength and unselfish devotion to family and friends during her long lifetime. She outlived my father by thirteen years.

My father's mother, Gudbjorg Hannesdottir, made her home with us always, in fact my father and her were only apart three to four months during their lifetimes. She it was who taught my father to read and write. She was an artist with her knitting needles. She taught herself to read and understand English, although she had no association with English speaking people.

Then always a stones throw away, lived my aunt, Sigurlaug, my father's only sister. She was a woman of great strength of character and capabilities. She performed midwifery for several years. With her dark eyes and black hair, she reflected foreign ancestry in the family.

Let us reflect for a few moments on the lives of these women.

My main purpose in appearing before you here today is to endeavor to express my gratitude for the monumental task which is about to take place here. I cannot find words that will adequately express what I feel. To the Icelandic Union of Farmers who came long distances and contributed so generously to this project, somehow I feel that this must be an unparalleled event for the Icelandic Societies of Calgary and Edmonton. My gratitude to the Alberta Restoration Foundation, who will carry out this gigantic project and lastly to this community of Markerville who have cooperated and worked so tirelessly towards this project. I say on behalf of the family and myself, please accept our deepest gratitude. May all your future ventures prosper and may you be richly rewarded.

I feel I have indeed been priviledged to have been born and raised in this community, in our wonderful land, Canada and especially do I appreciate the fact that my parents chose Alberta as my birthplace.

Thank you.

In May of 1976, a year after the Dedication, the Alberta Government officially declared Stephansson House an historic site.[5] They immediately began the process of buying the property. In August the site was purchased from the Leif Eiriksson Club of Calgary, which had aquired it in 1975. The price was $2,239, just enough for the club to recover its costs.[6] On hearing about the designation, Rosa wrote a heartfelt letter to the Minister of Culture, Horst Schmid.

Red Deer, Alberta
Aug. 14th 1976

Hon. Horst Schmid,
Edmonton, Alta.

Dear Sir,

Recently I received an interesting notice from your Department, to the effect that my parental home, the Stephansson house at Markerville, had been declared a Historic Site. I feel so privileged to have lived to witness this great event taking place, and am very deeply touched.

It is a great source of satisfaction to think that the contribution my parents made towards the cultural life of this area, is recognised by this generation. I feel that this will add a very interesting feature to the posterity of this community. People will be able to come and spend an inspirational and relaxing period of time, in this quiet spot.

I extend my most grateful thanks to all concerned, who assisted in the culmination of this great project, and to you in particular.

I have one note to add. My father only made one trip to Iceland, in 1917, when at the invitiation of the Icelandic Government he spent a summer travelling on horseback, through the countryside. Incidentally the Young Peoples Clubs in Iceland were the instigators of that idea. I would also like to say, that my father wrote the numerous poems he composed in Alberta, in his study, which he had built shortly after the turn of the century. Their bedroom [Stephan and Helga's] was an alcove of the study — which made it convenient for 'Wakeful Nights'. [The name of a volume of Stephan G.'s poetry]

Thanking you again and wishing for you great success in your future endeavors, for our wonderful province.

Respectfully Yours,
Rosa S. Benediktson[7]

Although the decision had finally been made to restore the house, it took some time to begin the work. Ten thousand dollars had been donated for the project by the Icelandic Farmers Union at the dedication ceremony in 1975, but the stabilization of the house did not begin until the summer of 1978. In spite of some negative initial reports on the condition of the house, the project moved ahead. As-found drawings and restoration plans were made, the roof was sealed, and the building was properly ventilated to prevent moisture build-up.[8] The next year, in 1979, the real restoration work began.[9]

Stephansson House before restoration, ca. 1978

Rosa's main contribution to the project was as a member of the Restoration Committee. At the 1975 Dedication Ceremony, the Icelandic Farmers' Union had generously donated $10,000 for the restoration of the house. Al Arnason, the Icelandic Consul for Alberta, set up the committee to dispense those funds and to lobby the government to take on the restoration.[10]

Once the committee had succeeded in getting government support, they worked closely with members of the Historic Sites Service to see the project through to completion. The province paid for the bulk of the building restoration, while the original donation went towards the restoration and aquisition of furniture for the home.[11] All of the furniture that had been moved to the University of Manitoba was returned to the home, except for Stephan G.'s book shelf and books.[12] In a letter to her son, Stephan V., Rosa relates some of the details discussed at one Restoration Committee meeting.

Monday morning,
Nov. 24th 1980

Dear Stephan & Family,

[preceeded by general news] ....On Sat. this Committee which is associated with the Historic Sites re[:] the old house, met at my place & had a long meeting. There were 2 from Calg. [Calgary] 4 from Edm. [Edmonton] & Joe & Shirley here. They were making arrangements for the disposal of the $11,000 plus interest, which was donated towards the restoration of the old house, from the farmers in Iceland and others. They donated $10,000 & there was another $1000 from another fund & the interest amounts to quite a bit more. So it was a busy week.

The historic sites has big plans re[:] the establishment of a Park area around the house & they want to buy 32 acres more, so that the old place won't be surrounded by acreages & houses & then they will develop a parking lot & scenic route past Markerville etc.etc. & on to the Highway. I just learned this now from Mrs. McCracken [Ross]. That

They will be looking for students to work at the site next summer to guide and instruct tourists. Where is Susan [Stephan's daughter] going to be and what will she be doing? This is what they plan on doing. Even though they won't be finished with the renovation they want to open it to the public, to let them see what they have been doing. They have a lot of work to do yet. They were shovelling the shingles off, one man at work, when we were there about 2 wks. ago. They have all the siding off, & the old rotten logs replaced & a concrete beam under the house & I guess a furnace room. Such a big task! The shingles are there, also the new siding. Lucky to have such good weather, so they can still work outside....

Bye for now.
Love Mum.

A meeting of the Stephansson House Restoration Committee

Standing: Al Arnason, Cliff Marteinsson, Joe Johansson In front: Thordis Gutnick, Rosa, Jane Ross

In Rosa's letter she talks about the purchasing of additional land around the house. The land in question belonged to Mundi's son, Edwin Stephenson (alternate spelling). Edwin, who had bought the homestead from Jake, had been willing to sell the house and some land to the province. Negotiations for the additional land north of the house began about the time of Rosa's letter, but Edwin was reluctant to sell. From the beginning, he had felt that he might lose some of his privacy by having a tourist attraction next to his home. The province offered to buy the land and lease it back to him, in addition to building a privacy fence, but he did not want to give up ownership of his family land. Having thwarted the government's efforts, Edwin has remained on the property to this day. [13]

The house during restoration, ca. 1981

It was decided by the Historic Sites Service that the house would be restored to the way it appeared in 1927, the year of Stephan G.'s death. A report was written by the Facility Director, Joan McKinnon, and Research Officer, Jane McCraken (now Jane Ross), in 1981. It described some of the findings of the restorers regarding the sequence of construction of the house, and also provided detailed furnishing specifications. The following excerpts give some insight into the original construction.

> *The evidence indicates that a five meter square dovetailed log home was built on the knoll overlooking the Medicine River but whether this was the original log house that Stephansson built the autumn of 1889 is not known. At some point, a log lean-to was attached to the east wall of this house. With a family of three adults, three children and twin baby girls, this first home soon proved to be too small. The arrival of Gestur in the*

spring of 1893 forced Stephansson to expand his house. Writing to a friend, Stephan asked him to pick up a blank permit for "house logs" so he could legally fell timbers on crown land for the contemplated addition to his home. How large the addition was at that time is unknown but in 1897-98 he wrote: " I didn't have a roof over my head. I was tearing down my old house and building it up again." This might have been a reference to a large L-shaped addition, again of log, that was built onto the south and west walls of the original house. A second storey over part of this addition was built at the same time, and horizontal drop siding nailed over the logs.

This addition tripled the living space in the Stephansson home. But within a few years with the arrival of the last of the eight children, Rosa, even this addition proved too restrictive. Undertaking a major expense, Stephansson dismantled the log lean-to on the east wall to replace it with a frame constructed addition which extended beyond the front of the house. A framed bay window was added to the study and a verandah was built across part of the front of the house. Thus, by 1907, the Stephansson house was basically complete. Although no crest work decorated the roofline as was so common of the period, Stephansson incorporated enough elements – the verandah, the bay window, the latticework, decorative window mouldings, the upstairs dormer – to make his home a picturesque Victorian cottage.

....Nothing is known of the utilization of the space in the home prior to the construction of the framed addition on the east side of the house. It is only after 1907 when the house assumed its final form that information is available from Rosa Bendiktson....[14]

Some of the information provided by Rosa can be found in her address "My Old Home". In it she describes not only the appearance of the house and how some of the rooms were used, but she also gives some details about the atmosphere of her childhood home.

My Old Home
Rosa - no date

Rosa reminiscing in her father's study

On looking back over my shoulder, so as to speak, I can observe my childhood home as it was in my earliest memories. That picture is identical to the photograph which was taken in August 1907. My father chose the location for the home when he first came out to the settlement in the spring of 1889. This land was actually my paternal grandmother's homestead. Being a widow, she had the privilege to acquire a quarter [section] of land. She made her home with my parents all her life.

Father, on the other hand, chose for his homestead, hay land, some three miles to the northeast. Here he built a log house, where the family resided in 1900 for a short period of time . This house was later moved down to the first location where it served as a horse barn and chicken house for years, only recently the last vestige of it was demolished.

In all likelihood my father first built the main log house with an upstairs in it. It was always referred to as the "Big Room". It had a front door facing south and double windows. Along the east side, was the kitchen, with a small area partitioned off on the north side, to serve as a pantry. There were four windows to the east. On the south end a bedroom was built for my sisters, whilst the boys slept upstairs. The girls bedroom had one window to the south.

North of the "Big Room" an addition was made exclusively for my grandmother. Here was her bedroom, with a space to do her handicrafts. Part of the room was partioned off, and here was a square iron heater. There were two windows, one facing west and one north, also two doors, one to the kitchen and one to the main room.

The last addition to the house was my father's study or "Small Room", as he termed it – although it was a fair sized room. It was built west of the "Big Room" and a small area was partioned off on the northern end, which was my parents bedroom. It had double windows to the west, and a bay window on the south, with three windows. So the room was well lit, and the scene to the west was a panoramic view of the Rocky Mountain Range, with the Medicine River just below the house. During the ensuing years the forests have grown tall, so now the peaks are scarcely visible.

A veranda was built on the south side over the front door, and the double windows, with some decorations like, lattice work on the top and on the lower edge, extending around the bay window. There was some fret work on the posts for decoration, and over the upstairs window was a half moon. My second oldest brother [Mundi] assisted my father no doubt, with the building, as he became a skilled carpenter early in life.

The entire house was built of logs, with the exception of the latest addition, namely, my father's study – it was built from lumber. The interior was finished, in the then popular V joint, with the exception of the kitchen, and the Big Room – it had linoleum on the walls, which is still there. The whole house was finished on the outside with siding, and was painted white with green trimmings.

Underneath the bay window, wild Alberta roses were planted, and they bloomed profusely for years. One day my mother brought home a root of a hops climber, and planted it beside the verandah. It grew well, and covered the entire front, and even climbed to the very top of the roof. A friend of my fathers, who was a gardener in Duluth, Minnesota, sent him some lilacs and shrubs, shortly after the turn of the century. They are still there, which testifies to their longevity. My father and brothers planted large numbers of spruces, out to the road, and all around the house, except to the west, and later more were added.

The house was heated with small heaters in the rooms, but in my fathers study was a large oval iron heater. I can recollect how I liked to sit in the dark beside it, on a winters night, while my father sat in his big chair chanting poetry, in a low voice. Later my father installed central heating, which was a great improvement. The kitchen was cold on wintery nights, for the fuel was wood, which burned up rapidly.

The house was roomy, and there was need for it, for the household was often quite large. As the first school in the district Hola, was erected in 1892, just east of our home, several young people – who lived some distance away – stayed at my parents home for a period of time, in order to acquire a bit of education. My two brothers [Baldur and Mundi] made their home with my parents when they were first married, for awhile. I remember others who stayed with us for periods of time, when their circmstances were difficult for one reason or other. Being always close to a school quite a number of school teachers boarded at our place. There was often much gaiety with so many young people around.

Our old home was always blessed with alot of company. Neighbors dropped in when they were coming or going to the village, as they knew how pleased father was to get the mail. They had time to stop and chat and of course my mother was always at hand with coffee. Then there were visitors from far away places. I can recall many distinguished guests from Iceland, and from other distant places. They desired to meet my father personally, and for him it was a spiritually uplifting experience to make their aquaintance, I feel certain.

To me it is of immeasurable value to have these pleasant memories of my parental home. It was always so homelike and comfortable, and I felt so secure, for my parents were always there. I consider myself so fortunate to have had it, and that I was brought up in that era of time. My father made a deep impact on the home with his wisdom and steadfast equanimity, and my mother was ever at his side with her light heartedness and deep concern for home and family. Blessed be the memory of my parents, and blessed be the memory of my parental home.

**Stephansson House after restoration
(the siding was painted magenta,
and the trim, light green)**

Although Rosa was delighted with the overall restoration of the house, there was one issue that always troubled her. She was very unhappy with the paint colours used for the exterior. Rosa remembered the house as being a light beige, and did not agree with the magenta siding and light green trim chosen by the government restorers. Many letters on this subject were sent back and forth between the family and the researchers.[15] The following letter was sent to Stephan Benediktson from the Minister of Culture only a week before the official opening, in an effort to explain the government's position. The house was being restored to its appearance in 1927. In spite of their arguments, Rosa, who had lived in the house until 1928, remained steadfast in her view that the house had never been painted so brightly.

July 30, 1982...

Dear Mr. [Stephan] Benediktson,

In reply to your message of July 26, 1982, concerning the colour of the exterior of Stephansson House, Alberta Culture researched the colour very carefully and checked numerous times to ensure the accuracy. As you know, Stephansson House has been restored to 1927, the year of your grandfather's death. This date was chosen so that all of Stephansson's publications and gifts that he received on his speaking tours could be displayed in the house.

When determining the colour of the exterior of the house, no true beige paint was found on the present structure. During the course of restoration cream paint samples [were] taken, but they were found above the present kitchen ceiling, indicating that the house was painted that colour prior to when the kitchen roof was raised. Mrs. Rosa Benediktson has told Historic sites staff that her father raised the kitchen roof circa 1914. Once Stephansson raised the roof, he had to re-paint his home and the colours he chose were magenta and green.

The as-found drawings and notes taken by [the] Historic Sites restoration team indicate that the house was indeed painted these colours. Paint samples taken from the soffit and siding showed the same colour combination. The exact shade of magenta was easily determined when a can of the original powder paint was located at the home of Edwin Stephansson. The powder was first mixed with water and a magenta colour resulted. This colour closely matches the paint remaining on the siding and therefore matches the paint when it was originally applied to the house. The powder was then mixed with a small amount of hydrochloric acid to determine the presence of red lead pigment. Small flecks of white which appeared indicated that the pigment is in the powder.

The above physical evidence, of course, conflicts with oral testimony almost all of which was gathered from people recalling the house as it appeared in the 1930s and 1940s. The reason for the discrepancy lies in the type of paint, for red lead when exposed to light fades. The beige colour remembered by your family was without doubt, the magenta which had faded. However, fading was uneven: on exposed faces, the red pigment faded quickly to a light pink and then beige. But in the protected areas under the eaves and the ceiling of the verandah the original magenta colour remained up to the time of restoration. It is standard practice, in cases of faded surfaces, to paint the restored structure the original colour as that is the only shade of which there is any certainty.

It is unfortunate that your family is upset with the colour of the house, for we have enjoyed a good working relationship throughout this project. The recent press coverage has been most favourable with no adverse comment on the colour. Further in support of our decision on the paint, a number of visitors from the district recall the magenta.

On behalf of the Premier and myself, I assure you that historical accuracy is always first priority in the restoration of our historic sites and I trust that this letter adequately explains the reasons for the colour of the house.

Yours sincerely,
Mary J. LeMessier [16]

In spite of the differences in opinion, the official opening of Stephansson House went ahead on August 7, 1982. A letter from the Deputy Minister inviting Rosa to take part in the ceremony also describes some of the events of the day.

July 13, 1982...

Dear Mrs. Benediktson,

On behalf of the honourable Mary J. LeMessier, Minister of Culture for Alberta, it is my pleasure to request your presence at a ceremony to be held at Stephansson House provincial historic site near Markerville, Alberta, on August 7, 1982. Mr. Ingvar Gislason, Minister of Culture and Education for Iceland will be in attendance as the guest of honour. As well, there will be approximately two hundred Icelanders, including a group which donated funds towards the restoration of the House.

On this date, the restored home of the famous Icelandic Canadian poet, Stephan G. Stephansson, will be officially opened to the public. The ceremony will commence at 2:00 p.m. on the lawn in front of the House. We would be grateful if you would agree to attend, as a member of the platform party, to give a tribute to your mother, Helga. Following the dedication of the House, we would ask that you accompany the Minister of Culture for Alberta and Iceland's Minister of Culture and Education from the platform to the House to cut the ribbon to officially open this important site.

A program for this event will be printed shortly and your response to this invitation, as soon as possible, would be welcome. If, as we hope, you will be able to attend, a short biographical sketch would assist the Chairman to introduce you as part of the platform party.

I look forward to your reply and hope that you will be able to favour our request.

Sincerely,
J.S. O'Neill
Deputy Minister [17]

The event was a great success. Thanking the minister in a brief letter, Rosa stated that "August 7th was just a wonderful experience in my life. Everything seemed to work out so well, and Nature did her best too!" Two days later, on August 9th, the *Red Deer Advocate* ran a front page story.

National pride in the accomplishments of a native son brought a planeload of people all the way from Iceland for the official opening Saturday of the Stephansson House.

About 700 people – most of them of Icelandic descent – made the pilgrimmage to the small pioneer home 15 km west of Red Deer where Icelandic poet Stephan Gudmundsson Stephansson homesteaded in [1889] and where he died in 1927.

....Mr. Stephansson is held in such esteem in his homeland that 230 people chartered a plane from Iceland. The planeload included Iceland's Minister of Culture and Education Ingvar Gislason and Ingi Tryggvason, president of the Iceland Farmer's Union which donated $10,000 to the restoration of Stephansson House.[18]

**Rosa at the opening ceremony
with Minister of Culture,
Mary J. LeMessier**

The Later Years

Following her retirement in 1968, Rosa was finally able to take some time for her own enjoyment. Over the next twenty years she travelled extensively, visiting family and friends all over the world. Along with her growing role as a speaker and community representative, she kept very busy with a wide range of activities from swimming to choral music. Her family was, of course, her greatest interest, and she spent as much time with her children and grandchildren as she could. As with everything else in her life, Rosa kept notebooks filled with accounts of her travels. She also saved pamphlets, letters, menus, and other souvenirs from her adventures.

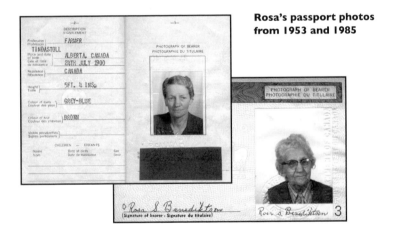

Rosa's passport photos from 1953 and 1985

Even before her retirement, Rosa had taken a few trips. On her many vacations, she took nearly every type of transportation available, and was never timid about tackling long journeys. In 1963 she flew to Whitehorse to visit Conrad and Linda. She returned to the Yukon in July of 1966, accompanied by her friend Josie Janssen. This time they travelled to Whitehorse by bus. On the return trip, they took the train to Juneau, a ship to Vancouver, and a plane back to Edmonton. Rosa arrived home just in time for Ted's wedding to Ruth on July 20th.

Two years later, in September of 1968, Rosa had the opportunity to visit Australia. She travelled with Stephan, Audrey, and their two children, who were returning to their home in Melbourne. Her journey back to Canada was by sea, where she spent nearly a month aboard the *Canberra*, a luxury cruise liner. The ship made stops in Sydney, Auckland, Samoa, Honolulu, and Vancouver. Although she enjoyed her adventure, she later told Stephan that she was glad to get off the ship in Vancouver.[1]

Rosa with grandchildren Steve and Susan in Australia, 1968

Rosa loved to visit her children and grandchildren wherever they were. After Con and Linda's return to Alberta in 1966, she accompanied them on family vacations in their motorhome.[2] In 1971, she again went north by bus, this time to visit Ted and Ruth and their first son. They were living in Yellowknife, NWT. The following year she boarded a train and travelled across Canada to see Stephan's family, who had moved to Ottawa. Fortunately for Rosa, Iris and Alfred and their five children remained in Alberta and she was able to see them a little more often.

In 1974, Rosa was delighted to be able to return to Iceland. She and her niece, Ethel Stephansson Rawlinson, of Idaho, joined a tour organized by the Vancouver Icelandic Society. They were to take part in the celebrations for the 1,100 year anniversary of the colonization of Iceland. In a speech that Rosa gave a year later at the Icelandic Picnic in Markerville, she recounted her trip in detail. The following excerpts touch on some of the highlights.

....I was very busy receiving phone calls, visiting old friends and meeting new ones. My niece and I were invited to many dinner parties by relatives and friends. I visited museums, galleries and the National Library. There I enjoyed leafing through my father's old manuscripts which I had seen him preparing for publication when I was a child of eight. He sat up many a night writing them with his painstaking exactness. My mother would get up during the night and brew him some coffee. It was like meeting old friends to see these manuscripts once again.

....On Friday the 19th of July we were in the area where my parents came from, Skagafjord. By some strange coincidence, we were at the cenotaph, which had been erected for my father's centennial in 1953 on exactly the same day as I had been there 21 years previously. We stopped and were able to take pictures. For me it was a touching moment.

Rosa revisiting the Cenotaph in Iceland with her niece Ethel, 1974

Even after she turned eighty, Rosa was still travelling. In 1981, Stephan and Audrey took her on a trip to the Icelandic Festival of Manitoba, in Gimli. For several years they had wanted to visit the festival together. After their trip, Rosa and Audrey returned to Calgary, while Stephan went back to Abu Dhabi to finish his work there.[3]

**Audrey and Rosa at the
Icelandic Festival in Gimli**

At eighty-two years of age Rosa went to Disneyland. Never afraid of a challenge, she hopped on a bus with her nephew Cecil's widow, Dolly Stephansson, for a two-week trip to California and Arizona. While on this particular adventure, she took only brief notes; however, she did describe the tour of Los Angeles and some of the rides and shows at Disneyland, commenting that [we] "went on a lot of rides including some like at [the] Seattle World's Fair." Rosa's last big trip was in 1985, when she went to visit Stephan's family, now in Argentina. She flew to Buenos Aires, where she stayed for a month. She was eighty-four years old.

Rosa always had a remarkably positive attitude about her lot in life, as well as a great sense of humor. When she turned eighty, the usually shy and reserved Rosa wrote a very amusing piece on what it was like to reach that age. It's not clear to whom it was written, but it certainly shows her mischievous side.

We oldsters sure do get away with a lot just because we've managed to keep breathing longer than most folks. I've just celebrated my eightieth birthday and I've got it made.

If you forget someone's name or an appointment or what you said yesterday, just explain that you are eighty, and you will be forgiven. If you spill soup on someone's dress, or forget to put your dentures in, or take some other woman's gloves by mistake, or put your wig on backwards, Just say, "I'm eighty you know", and no one will say a word.

You have a perfect alibi for everything when you are eighty. If you act silly, you are in your second childhood.

Being eighty is much better than being seventy. At seventy people are mad at you for everything, but if you make it to eighty, you can talk back, argue, disagree and insist on having your own way because everyone thinks you are getting a little soft in the head.

They say that life begins at forty. Not true. If you ask me life begins at 80.

Sign[ed] me – Got it made at 80

At about that time, Rosa finally had to move out of the house that she had bought from Con and Linda over twenty years before.[4] Adjusting to life in her new home in a seniors' apartment took some time, but she did ultimately develop a very active social life and took part in many activities. In a letter to Stephan in 1981 she describes her schedule for the week.

I think I'll go swimming next Wed. & I'm singing with the choir, and am going to the Drama Class, & am reporter for the C.V.P., for a small paper which comes out monthly. Then there are other things going like Bingo Mon. nites, Cards Wed. nites & Shuffleboard Thurs. nite. Haven't been to a dance in months tho. I'm not enthused with some of these things, but go anyway.

Rosa belonged to the Golden Circle Choir, which performed in and around Red Deer. In an undated letter to her son Stephan, she tells him how her father had wanted her to sing when she was young.

We had a lovely concert at the United Church here yesterday. [Seven] Choirs of Sr. Citizens took part, including ours, the "Golden Circle Choir". It was lovely. I enjoy the choir so much. My father wanted me to sing in a choir, which was started in 1911 by a noted Icelandic musician [Professor Sigurd Helgason] in Markerville at that time. He lived there a short while, and left his mark because he started the Markerville Band, with the Icel. farm boys, who didn't know a note of music from a fly speck, or very few did. It flourished and operated for yrs. with great success. As I said Dad wanted me to be in the choir, but tells mother in 1911, how it is impossible to get me to do it. He had no idea how bashful his youngest was!! That was the sole reason. I loved singing & could learn a tune very quickly. My mother sang very well, but Dad was not a singer but when it came to lyrics, there he was quite at home and made them to some of the old tunes of the day!! Interesting! Many things to reflect on.

Sadly, over the next ten years, Rosa's health deteriorated. She was moved out of her apartment, first to a facility in Bashaw to be near Iris and Con's families.[5] Later, she lived with Stephan and Audrey in Calgary, until they found a place for her at the Bethany Care Centre in Cochrane.[6] It was while living there, that she turned ninety. A small birthday party was held, at Stephan's home near Cochrane, and the event was marked by a telegram from the Historic Sites Service.

To Rosa Benediktson

On behalf of Alberta Culture and Multiculturalism, I would like to extend our sincere congratulations and best wishes on the occasion of your 90th birthday.

The Stephansson family's contributions to, and enrichment of the multicultural fabric of Alberta's heritage is commemorated in the Stephansson House Provincial Historic Site and remains a legacy for all Albertans to enjoy.

Dr. Frits Pannekoek,
Acting Assistant Deputy Minister,
Historic Sites Service,
Alberta Culture and Multiculturalism.

Rosa's 90th birthday
at Stephan's home
near Cochrane

Rosa's later years were also marked by extreme sadness. Two terrible tragedies befell the family with the unexpected deaths of Rosa's youngest sons, Ted and Conrad. "Sigurdur Theodor Oliver Benediktson known to all of his friends as 'Ted' passed away suddenly on January 11, 1989 in Vancouver B.C. at age 46 years."[7] Ted had suffered a sudden heart attack. Only a year and half later, on October 4, 1991, Conrad Benedikt Jon Benediktson also had a heart attack and passed away. He was only fifty-four.

Rosa had sufferered a great deal of loss in her life, but the premature passing of her husband and two sons was truly heartbreaking. On December 26, 1995, four years after Conrad's death, Rosa herself died quietly in her sleep. She was ninety-five years of age. At the time of her death the matriarch of the Benediktson family had twelve grandchildren, fifteen great grandchildren and one great-great grandchild. Among all of her many contributions and accomplishments, this was Rosa's greatest legacy. Her daughter Iris tried, in two brief pages, to express her love and admiration for her mother.

Remembering My Mother

My mother Rosa S. (Stephansson) Benediktson was a very special kind of person. She was very articulate but quite shy, and often felt inadequate to the job she was expected to perform. As she got older and traveled more, her self confidence gained greatly. She was widowed after only fourteen years of marriage, losing her partner and the person she loved and admired, I should say, possibly adored more than life itself. Her faithfulness to my Dad lasted her whole life and she made it quite clear to all of us, that's the way it was. My three brothers and myself never felt deprived of anything even though the first few years after my Dad's sudden death were pretty lean.

Mother was true socialist and counted among her very good friends, Grant Notley, Alberta's leader of the New Democratic Party, and felt his family's loss as Alberta's loss at his untimely death.

Mother and I were at the extremes in our political thinking but, though her outward feelings were often well hidden, she told me she was proud of my political efforts during the eighties. We as a family have all inherited her basic integrity and learned to share and reach for higher horizons than any of us even imagined we could reach.

Thank you Mother for all you gave us.

Rosa and Iris

Rosa's contributions to the adopted home of her parents continue to this day. 2003 is the 150th anniversary of the birth of Stephan G. Stephansson. Rosa's work in preserving his literary legacy has allowed the continued study and publication of his poetry, as well as an increased understanding of the history of the Western Icelanders. The Stephansson House Provincial Historic site still attracts between four and five thousand visitors annually.[8] In 1988, The Rosa Benediktson Prize in Comparative Literature was established at the University of Alberta. It is "given to a third year student in the Honors or Specialization Program in Comparative Literature, who shows excellence in academic work and community involvement".[9] The Stephansson family values of education, hard work, and community service have been richly rewarded.

At Close of Day [10]
Stephan G. Stephansson

When sunny hills are draped in velvet shadows
  By summer night
And Lady Moon hangs out among the tree tops
  Her crescent bright;
And when the welcome evening breeze is cooling
  My fevered brow
And all who toil rejoice that blessed night time
  Approaches now –

When out among the herds the bells are tinkling
  Now clear, now faint,
As in the woods a lonely bird is voicing
  His evening plaint;
The wandering breeze with drowsy accent whispers
  Its melody,
And from the brook the joyous cries of children
  Are borne to me;

When fields of grain have caught a gleam of moonlight
  But dark the ground –
A pearl-grey mist has filled to over-flowing
  The dells around;
Some golden stars are peeping forth to brighten
  The eastern wood –
Then I am resting out upon my doorstep
  In nature's mood.

My heart reflects the rest and sweet rejoicing
    Around, above;
Where beauty is the universal language
    And peace and love.
Where all things seem to join in benediction
    And prayers for me;
Where at night's loving heart both earth and heaven
    At rest I see.

And when the last of all my days is over,
    The last page turned –
And, whatsoever shall be deemed in wages
    That I have earned,
In such a mood I hope to be composing
    My sweetest lay –
And then extend my hand to all the world
    And pass away

This was one of Rosa's favorite poems, written by her father in 1883. It was read at her memorial service by Iris.

(translated by Jakobina Johnson)

Family Tree

Stephan's Family

Gudmundur Stefansson
m. **Gudbjorg Hannesdottir**
b. July 8, 1830 - d. January 12, 1911

Daughter - Sigurlaug Einara
b. November 19, 1860

Son **- Stefan Gudmundsson**
b. October 3, 1853
- d. Aug. 10, 1927

Helga's Family

Sigurbjorg Stefansdottir
(half-sister of G. Stefansson)
m. Jon Jonsson

Daughter **- Helga Sigridur
Jonsdottir** b. July 3, 1859
- d. December 12, 1940

Son - Jon Jonsson

**Stefan Gudmundsson (Stephan Gudmundson Stephansson)
m. Helga Sigridur Jonsdottir,** August 28, 1878

Son - Baldur b. September 25, 1879 - d. June 13, 1949

Son - Gudmundur (Mundi) b. December 9, 1881- d. March 4, 1947

Son - Jon b. 1883, d. 1887

Son - Jakob (Jake) Kristinn b. June 8, 1886 - d. March 21, 1959

Twin Daughters
- Stephany (Fanny) Gudbjorg b. October 6, 1889 - d. December 17, 1940
- Jona (Jennie) Sigurbjorg b. October 6, 1889 - d. June 24, 1969

Son - Gestur Cecil b. May 31, 1893 - d. July 16, 1909

Daughter **- Rosa Siglaug b. July 24, 1900 - d. December 26, 1995**

June 17, 1928, Rosa Siglaug Stephansson
- m. Sigurdur Vilberg Gudmundsson Benediktson
  b. May 14, 1901 - d. November 14, 1942

Daughter - Helga **Iris** b. November 1, 1929 - m. Alfred Bourne, April 28, 1947

       Daughter - Elsie Marie b. February 13, 1948

       Daughter - Margo Patricia b. December 10, 1949

       Son - William Sigurd b. March 28, 1954

       Son - Thomas Rodger b. June 10, 1957

       Son - James Alfred b. April 8, 1968

Son - **Stephan** Vilberg b. June 22, 1933 - m. Audrey Jones, December 1, 1956 (divorced)
- m. Adriana Kroes, November 24, 1995

       Son - Stephan Robert b. September 28, 1957

       Daughter - Susan Rosa b. October 13, 1961

       Son - Paul David b. December 10, 1968

Son - **Conrad** Benedikt Jon b. April 28, 1937 - d. October 4, 1991
- m. Christina Linda Schultz, August 22, 1959

       Daughter - Darryce Christine b. July 30, 1963

       Son - Darryl Conrad b. February 22, 1965

Son - Sigurdur **Theodor** Olafur b. June 21, 1942 - d. January 11, 1989
- m. Ruth Metcalfe, July 20, 1966

       Son - Theodor Gordon Sigurdur b. Nov. 29, 1966

       Son - Derek Ramon b. July 16, 1974

Notes

Introduction

1. J.W. McCracken (1982a), p. 15.

The Journey

1. McCracken (1982a), p. 3.
2. Ibid., p. 6.
3. Ibid., p. 10.
4. J.W. McCracken (1982b), p. 36-39.
5. J.J. Hunford (1909), p.31-44.
6. Idem.
7. McCracken (1982a, p. 66).
8. Ibid., p. 68.

Childhood

1. S.V. Benediktson, personal communication, March 20, 2003.
2. McCracken (1982a), p. 71.
3. Ibid., p. 80.
4. R.J. Asgeirsson, personal communication, February 26, 2003.
5. *The Advance,* Aug 19, 1926.
6. R.S. Benediktson (1956).
7. S.V. Benediktson, personal communication, March 25, 2003.
8. V. Hreinsson, personal communication, May 20, 2003.
9. E. Anderson, personal communication, March 5, 2003.

The Olds School of Agriculture

1. E.B. Swindlehurst (1964?), p. 9.

2. *The A.S.A. Magazine* (1917), p. 42.

3. Swindlehurst, p. 24.

4. H.I. Bourne, personal communication, February 3, 2003.

5. Swindlehurst, p. 51.

6. *Alberta Provincial Schools of Agriculture Calendar for 1920-21* (1920), p. 21-22.

7. Ibid., p. 49.

8. Ibid., p. 56-57.

9. Translated by Erla Anderson.

10. Translated by Erla Anderson.

11. McCracken (1982a), p. 93.

12. *The A.S.A. Magazine* (1920).

13. *Alberta Provincial Schools of Agriculture Calendar for 1920-21*, p. 24.

14. *The A.S.A. Magazine* (1920).

Raising a Family

1. S.V. Benediktson (2002), p. 10.

2. Ibid., p. 10.

3. Idem.

4. H.I. Bourne (1987), p. 651.

5. Idem.

6. V. Galloway, personal communication, April 20, 2003.

7. S.V. Benediktson, p. 11.

8. Idem.

9. H.I. Bourne, p. 651.

10. Idem.

11. Idem.

12. S.V. Benediktson, p. 10.

13. Ibid., p. 12.

14. H.I. Bourne, personal communication, April 13, 2003.

15. S.V. Benediktson, personal communication, April 20, 2003.

16. S.V. Benediktson, p. 2.

17. Newpaper clipping from R. Benediktson's papers, source unknown. November, 1942.

18. S.V. Benediktson, p. 2.

19. Ibid., p. 13.

20. M. Chaumont, personal communication, April 21, 2003.

21. Ibid.

22. *Red Deer Advocate*, June 22, 1949.

23. S.V. Benediktson, p. 17.

24. Ibid., p. 18.

25. S.V. Benediktson, personal communication, February 24, 2003.

26. Ibid.

27. S.V. Benediktson, p. 24.

28. Ibid., p. 25.

29. H.I. Bourne, personal communication, April 21, 2003.

30. S.V. Benediktson, p. 27.

31. Ibid., p. 31.

32. Ibid., p. 33.

33. S.V. Benediktson, personal communication, February 24, 2003.

34. Ibid.

35. H.I. Bourne, personal communication, April 21, 2003.

36. Ibid.

Contribution to Community

1. R.S. Benediktson (1973)

2. Red Deer and District Archives, MG 208. Printed with the permission of the Vonin Ladies Aid.

3. B. Anderson, personal communication, April 21, 2003.

The Poet's Daughter

1. McCracken (1982a), p. 132-133.

2. *Red Deer Advocate*, July 22, 1936.

3. *Red Deer Advocate*, September 6, 1950.

4. Translated by Erla Anderson.

5. *Red Deer Advocate*, August 3, 1989.

6. Translated by Erla Anderson.

7. S.V. Benediktson, personal communication, March 25, 2003.

8. F. Gudmundsson (1982), p. 90.

9. Translated by Erla Anderson.

10. Translated by Erla Anderson.

11. J. Ross, personal communication, March 28, 2003.

Stephansson House Restoration

1. Gudmundsson, p. 90.

2. Alberta. Letter from B.A. Thorlakson to John Nicks, April 4, 1972. File on Stephansson House Restoration. Department of Community Development, Historic Sites and Cultural Facilities Branch.

3. *Red Deer Advocate*, August 11, 1975.

4. Idem.

5. Alberta. Press Release, May 20, 1976. File on Stephansson House Restoration.

6. Alberta. Letter from H. Schmidt to David J. Russell, August 13, 1976. File on Stephansson House Restoration.

7. Alberta. Letter from Rosa Benediktson to Horst Schmidt, August 14, 1976. File on Stephansson House Restoration.

8. Alberta. Memo from W.D. Clark to John Lunn, July 18, 1978. File on Stephansson House Restoration.

9. Alberta. Letter from Horst Schmidt to Kris K. Johnson, May 5, 1978. File on Stephansson House Restoration.

10. J. Ross, personal communication, March 28, 2003.

11. Idem.

12. V. Hreinsson, personal communication, May 20, 2003.

13. E. Stephenson, personal communication, April 1, 2003.

14. Alberta. Report: The Furnishing Specifications for the Stephansson House, May 1981. File on Stephansson House Furnishings. Department of Community Development, Historic Sites and Cultural Facilities Branch.

15. J. Ross, personal communication, March 28, 2003

16. Alberta. Letter from M.J. LeMessier to S.V. Benediktson, July 30, 1982. File on Stephansson House Restoration.

17. Alberta. Letter from J.S. O'Neill to Rosa Benediktson, July 13, 1982. File on Stephansson House Restoration.

18. *Red Deer Advocate*, August 9, 1982.

The Later Years

1. S.V. Benediktson, note on an unpublished typescript, Holidays 1966, by Rosa Benediktson.

2. L. Benediktson, personal communication, March 2003.

3. S.V. Benediktson, personal communication, April 13, 2003.

4. L. Benediktson, personal communication, March 2003.

5. Idem.

6. Idem.

7. *Red Deer Advocate*, January 14, 1989.

8. G. Duguay, personal communication, April 2003.

9. K. Gunnars. Letter to R. Benediktson, November 21, 1995.

10. McCracken (1982b), p. 30.

Bibliography

Alberta. Department of Community Development, Historic Sites and Cultural Facilities Branch (Edmonton). File on Stephansson House Restoration. Letter from B.A. Thorlakson to John Nicks, April 4, 1972.

Alberta. Department of Community Development, Historic Sites and Cultural Facilities Branch (Edmonton). File on Stephansson House Restoration. Press Release, May 20, 1976.

Alberta. Department of Community Development, Historic Sites and Cultural Facilities Branch (Edmonton). File on Stephansson House Restoration. Letter from H. Schmidt to David J. Russell, August 13, 1976.

Alberta. Department of Community Development, Historic Sites and Cultural Facilities Branch (Edmonton). File on Stephansson House Restoration. Letter from Rosa Benediktson to Horst Schmidt, August 14, 1976.

Alberta. Department of Community Development, Historic Sites and Cultural Facilities Branch (Edmonton). File on Stephansson House Restoration. Memo from W.D. Clark to John Lunn, July 18, 1978.

Alberta. Department of Community Development, Historic Sites and Cultural Facilities Branch (Edmonton). File on Stephansson House Restoration. Letter from Horst Schmidt to Kris K. Johnson, May 5, 1978.

Alberta. Department of Community Development, Historic Sites and Cultural Facilities Branch. File on Stephansson House Furnishings (Edmonton). Report: The Furnishing Specifications for the Stephansson House, May 1981.

Alberta. Department of Community Development, Historic Sites and Cultural Facilities Branch (Edmonton). File on Stephansson House Restoration. Letter from M.J. LeMessier to S.V. Benediktson, July 30, 1982.

Alberta. Department of Community Development, Historic Sites and Cultural Facilities Branch (Edmonton). File on Stephansson House Restoration. Letter from J.S. O'Neill to Rosa Benediktson, July 13, 1982.

The Advance, Wynyard, Saskatchewan, August 19, 1926

Alberta Provincial Schools of Agriculture Calendar for 1920-21 (1920). Edmonton, AB: The Board of Agricultural Education.

The A.S.A. Magazine (1917). Olds, AB: Agriculture Schools of Alberta.

The A.S.A. Magazine (1920). Olds, AB: Agriculture Schools of Alberta.

Benediktson, R.S. (1956). "Stephan G. Stephansson og Helga Jonsdottir" In F. Gudmundsson (Ed.) *Foreldrar minir* Endurminningar nokkurra Islendinga vestan hafs (p. 161-175). Reykjavik.

Benediktson, R.S. (1973). "Markerville Icelandic Ladies Aid (Vonin)" In *Grub-Axe to Grain* (p.133). Spruce View, AB: Spruce View School Area Historical Society.

Benediktson, S.V. (2002). *Stephan's Story: A Half Century in the International Oil Business*. Calgary, AB: Benson Ranch Inc.

Bourne, H.I. (1987). "Sigurdur Benediktson" In *Sod Shacks and Wagon Tracks* (p.651-653). Red Deer, AB: Big Pine Ridge Historical Society.

Gudmundsson, F. (1982). "A Few Treasured Belongings of the Stephan G. Stephansson Home Near Markerville, Alberta" In *Stephan G. Stephansson in Retrospect: Seven Essays* (p.90). Reykjavik: Icelandic Cultural Fund.

Hunford, Jonas J. (1909). "Stutt agrip af Landnamssogu Islendinga i Albertaheradi" *Almanak*, Olafs S. Thorgeirssonar ed.. Winnipeg, MB.

McCracken, J.W. (1982a). *Stephan G. Stephansson: the Poet of the Rocky Mountains*. Edmonton, AB: Alberta Culture, Historical Resources Division.

McCracken, J.W. (1982b). *Stephan G. Stephansson: Selected Translations from Andvokur*. Edmonton, AB: Stephan G. Stephansson Homestead Restoration Committee.

The Red Deer Advocate, July 22, 1936; June 22, 1949; September 6, 1950; August 11, 1975; August 9, 1982; January 14, 1989; August 3, 1989.

Swindlehurst, E.B. (1964?). *Alberta's Schools of Agriculture: A Brief History*. Edmonton, AB: Alberta Department of Agriculture.